Michael Hastings

LEE HARVEY OSWALD

*A Far Mean Streak of Indepence
Brought On by Negleck*

Penguin Books

Penguin Books Ltd, Harmondsworth, Middlesex, England
Penguin Books Inc., 3300 Clipper Mill Road, Baltimore 11. Md, U.S.A.
Penguin Books Australia Ltd, Ringwood, Victoria, Australia

—

First published in 1966
Copyright © Michael Hastings, 1966
All rights whatsoever in this play are strictly reserved and application for perform-
ance should be made to the author's agents, Jonathan Clowes Ltd, 20 New Cavendish
Street, London W1

—

Made and printed in Great Britain by
C. Nicholls & Company Ltd
Set in Monotype Baskerville

CONTENTS

'Lee Harvey Oswald was born in Oct 1939 in New Orleans, La. The son of a Insuraen Salesmen whose early death left a far mean streak of indepence brought on by negleck . . .'

'I wonder what would happen if somebody was to stand up and say he was utterly opposed not only to the governments, but to the people, to the entire land and complete foundations of his socially . . .'

'In the event of war, I would kill any american who put a uniform on in defence of the american government – any american.'

Two extracts, in the original spelling, from Oswald's Historic Diary, and an extract from a letter from Russia to his brother Robert.

CAST

SPEAKER

COMMISSION

MARINA, *Lee's wife*

MARGUERITE, *his mother*

LEE

Lee Harvey Oswald, A Far Mean Streak of Indepence Brought On by Negleck was first performed at the Hampstead Theatre Club, London, on the third anniversary of the assassination of President Kennedy, 22 November 1966, in a production directed by Peter Coe, designed by Michael Knights.

ACKNOWLEDGEMENTS

Much of this play could not have been compiled without the research and contribution to the subject that my fellow writers have made, and to whom I am indebted.

Thomas G. Buchanan, *Who Killed Kennedy?*, Secker & Warburg, 1964.

Fred J. Cook, 'The Oswald Case', *The Nation*, 1965.

Robert Donovan, 'Autopsy', *Los Angeles Times*, 30 May 1966.

Edward Jay Epstein, *Inquest: The Warren Commission and the Establishment of Truth*, Hutchinson, 1966.

Gerald R. Ford and John R. Stiles, *Portrait of the Assassin*, New York: Simon & Schuster, 1965.

Sylvan Fox, *The Unanswered Questions About President Kennedy's Assassination*, Award Books, 1965.

Nerin E. Gun, *Red Roses from Texas*, Muller, 1964.

John Clellon Holmes, 'The Silence of Oswald', Chicago: *Playboy*.

Joachim Joesten, *Oswald: Assassin or Fall Guy?*, Merlin Press, 1964.

Fletcher Knebel, 'The Oswald Mystery', *Look*, 12 July 1966.

Mark Lane, 'Brief for Oswald', *National Guardian*, 19 December 1963.

Mark Lane, *Rush to Judgment*, Bodley Head, 1966.

Dwight Macdonald, 'A Critique of the Warren Report', New York: *Esquire*, March 1965.

Sylvia Meagher, *An Independently Prepared Index to the Volumes of the Warren Commission Report*, New York: Scarecrow Press, 1966.

George and Patricia Nash *et al.*, *Critical Reactions to the Warren Report*, New York: Marzani & Munsell, 1964.

Richard R. Popkin, 'The Second Oswald', *New York Review*, 28 July 1966.

Vincent J. Salandria, 'The Minority of One', *The Nation*, 1965.

Vincent J. Salandria, 'The Warren Report', New York: *Liberation*, March 1965.

Merriman Smith *et al.*, *Four Days*, New York: United Press International and American Heritage, 1964.

Jean Stafford, *A Mother in History*, Chatto & Windus, 1966.

Harold Weisberg, *Whitewash*, Hyattstown, Maryland: Harold Weisberg, 1966.

'The Oswald Case' and 'Mrs Marguerite Oswald', Broadside Folkways Records, 1965.

Bob Considine and Dorothy Kilgallen of the *New York Journal American*.

Richard Dudman of the *St Louis Post Dispatch*.

Harold Feldman of *The Nation*.

Jack Minnis and Staughton Lynd of *The New Republic*.

Gene Roberts of the *Detroit Free Press*.

Leo Sauvage of *Le Figaro*.

Richard Starnes of the *New York World Telegram and Sun*.

PRESIDENT'S COMMISSION ON THE ASSASSINATION OF PRESIDENT KENNEDY

Chief Justice Earl Warren, Chairman
Senator Richard B. Russell
Senator John Sherman Cooper
Representative Hale Boggs
Representative Gerald R. Ford
Mr Allen W. Dulles
Mr John J. McCloy

J. Lee Rankin, General Counsel

Established by President Lyndon B. Johnson
29 November 1963

Report of the President's Commission on the Assassination of President John F. Kennedy (Warren Commission Report). 888 pages. Published 27 September 1964

Hearings Before the President's Commission on the Assassination of President Kennedy
26 volumes – Testimony and Exhibits. Published 23 November 1964

It must be stated clearly that all the passages between the Commission and the two witnesses are verbatim breakdowns of what actually took place. The performed scenes are the author's attempt to recreate Oswald's domestic past.

The play is an attempt to find Lee Harvey Oswald. There is no intended prejudice as to whether he killed Kennedy or not ·· that sort of inquiry still begs too much speculation to make for an unbiased rendering.

PROLOGUE

The stage is lit. On the stage hangs a white screen. There is a single stool. The backcloth is dark. The SPEAKER *walks out front. He sits. He talks* ...

SPEAKER: ... 1939, in New Orleans, Lee Harvey Oswald was born.[1] His father Robert had died two months before. Lee had an older half-brother,[2] by a previous marriage – his own brother was five years his senior.[3] Lee Oswald had a dog, he collected stamps and played chess and truant. Given probation for his frequent truancy, a social worker's report suggested Oswald was a withdrawn and maladjusted boy. The relationship between mother and son was tense. Aged sixteen he wrote to the Socialist Party of America – 'I am a Marxist'. Aged sixteen he failed to join the Marine Corps Reserve; his mother would not let him falsify his age. He had to wait for his seventeenth birthday. For a whole year he lived for the day he could join up. In the Marine Corps he learnt radar and studied Russian. He still kept few friends. Then Oswald applied for a discharge – apparently his mother could not support herself at home. He received an 'undesirable discharge'.[4] He had also made an application to a school for philosophy and science in Switzerland.[5] Home again briefly, he gave his mother

1. 18 October 1939.
2. John Edward Pic.
3. Robert Oswald.
4. 13 September 1960.
5. Albert Schweitzer College, Churwalden, Switzerland. 19 March 1959.

15

a hundred dollars; six days later he was on a ship in New Orleans.[1] He wrote to his mother – 'Well I have booked passage on a ship to Europe, I would of had to sooner or later and I think its best I go now.' Le Havre, London, Helsinki, Moscow, and to Minsk, where he worked in a factory. Lee applied for Russian citizenship. He tried to renounce his passport. He fell in love with a girl,[2] she would not wed him, he married another. She was Marina Prusakova. She was nineteen. A baby daughter, June Lee, was born. They both decided to return to the States. The American Embassy loaned them cash,[3] and via Moscow, Minsk, Brest their train brought them to Holland. Across the Atlantic to New York,[4] from there they flew to Texas.[5] Lee Oswald was twenty-one.

These facts seem dull beside the tragic actions which followed. But the early years must be paraphrased – the sum of a man is in his waking.

The Oswalds stayed with friends. They moved from one room to one cold-water apartment to one room again and again. Lee Oswald took numerous jobs, he never ceased searching for congenial employment. The pattern of his life was the same – erratic, uncertain, he was unable to cope with the America to which he had come back.

He left for New Orleans[6] where he was involved in a strange enterprise. He printed leaflets which read HANDS OFF CUBA. He described himself as a branch

1. 20 September 1960. s.s. Marion Lykes.
2. Ella German.
3. $435 71c.
4. s.s. Maarsdam at Hoboken New Jersey. 13 June 1962.
5. 14 June 1962.
6. 5 August 1963.

of the Fair Play for Cuba Committee. He also be-
friended various anti-Castro refugees who were openly
plotting against the Cuban régime.[1] One day his
friends found him distributing his leaflets. They
attacked him. They were arrested, and Oswald was
jailed for a night. Why?

Later Lee and Marina separated. Marina lived
with a friend.[2] Lee left for Mexico City.[3] He applied
at the Cuban Embassy for an 'in-transit' visa to
permit him to travel to Russia via Cuba.[4] He was
advised to apply at the Russian Embassy, which he
did. He was told it would take time to arrange it. He
seemed upset and impatient. He stayed for a week,
then left for Texas.[5]

On October 18, he applied at the Book Depository
building, and the Superintendent Roy S. Truly hired
him in a temporary capacity.

One month later, President John F. Kennedy was
assassinated by gunfire in Dallas.

These are the barest facts of Oswald's life with the
least embellishments that can be contrived.

[*The lights change. The white screen is lit. The*
SPEAKER *uses a stick to mark areas.*]

... on Friday morning, 22 November 1963, the
President arrived with his party at Love Field,
Dallas.[6] The motorcade drove through downtown
Dallas towards the Trade Mart for a luncheon speech.

[*Film of the motorcade commences.*]

1. Carlos Bringuier. Rolando Paez. Celso Hernandez. Miguel
   Cruz.
2. Mrs Ruth Paine. Irving, Dallas.
3. 25 September 1963.
4. Warren Commission Report, pp. 280–82
5. 3 October 1963.
6. 11.40 a.m. Friday 22 November 1963.

…This is Dealey Plaza. The motorcade turns left on Houston Street into Elm Street.

[*A still of the scene is shown.*]

… This is the Book Depository store. Here is the sixth-floor window … The overpass … the car-port … the trees in front of the Depository building … the trees in front of the car-port … and the slightly rising knoll – here. The bullets began to hit the car here.

[1][*A still from the film of the shooting. The car is driving along slowly; the President smiles and waves. Before the first bullet hits, the frame freezes.*]

More than four hundred people were in or around Dealey Plaza when the assassination ocurred. Two hundred and sixty-six witnesses to the crime are known. Of these, ninety were asked from where did the shots come. Fifty-eight witnesses said that the shots came from the direction of the grassy knoll, to the right fore-front of the car; the other thirty-two witnesses said otherwise.

[*The film moves again. The bullets hit President Kennedy, Governor Connally, and the car. The car gathers speed and pulls away. The film shows the general chaos of Dealey Plaza. People running, standing, or lying on the ground.*]

Abraham Zapruder, with an 8 millimetre camera, filmed the actual shooting from the bank leading up to the grass knoll.

[*Still of scene.*]

Zapruder's film runs at 18.3 frames per second. The earliest possible moment a bullet from the Book Depository store could have hit the car with clear

1. The sequence from this point to the end of the first paragraph on p. 20 is interchangeable. It can be placed after Marina's line on p. 103, 'Yes I am convinced.'

view of the car is after frame 210, because up to that frame an oak tree obscures the view of the car from the sixth floor window.

[*Still of first shot.*]

The President was first hit at frame 225.[1] The Governor sitting in front of him was hit by a subsequent bullet. You see the President being hit first ...

[*Still.*]

Then you see Connally turn to his right to look behind him. He cannot see the President, so he turns to his left.

[*Still.*]

Then he too is hit.

[*Still.*]

The Zapruder film shows that Connally was hit between frames 230 and 240. Now, it is universally acknowledged that any bullet fired from the 6.5 millimetre Mannlicher-Carcano rifle which it is claimed Oswald fired that day, needs a minimum of 2.3 seconds between firing. These are the Warren Commission's findings using expert riflemen. But 2.3 seconds between bullets amounts to 42.09 frames on Zapruder's 8 millimetre film. What this amounts to is – no bullet from that gun, whether the first strike was fired at 210 frames or 225 frames – no bullet from that gun could hit again by frame 240 – when the Governor was struck. Governor Connally testified to the Commission that he heard the first bullet crack. By then it had reached its target. He turned to the right, then to the left, and then he was hit. He testified he could not hear the second bullet fire. Which is not surprising. The Governor and his wife testified to the best of their knowledge that Connally was hit by a second bullet.

1. *Hearings*, XVIII, p.26.

The Warren Commission maintain that one bullet and one bullet only hit the President and then simultaneously crashed into the Governor's ribs, splintered his right wrist and lodged in his left thigh. In all there were five bullet wounds, two on the President, three on the Governor; some kind of fragment starred the car's windshield, and a bullet two grains lighter than its normal weight was found inside the car; there was a bullet in the Governor's thigh, and one bullet, the first, had ranged down inside the President's body. A further bullet was found on Governor Connally's stretcher at the hospital. This might appear to sound as if more than three bullets were fired. But this is a point the Warren Commission have not denied. It is possible – they suggest that one bullet missed altogether. But the Zapruder film which *Life* magazine owns exclusive rights to, does make it all too clear that the first two bullets could not have been fired from that one gun, the 6.5 millimetre Mannlicher-Carcano. That gun cannot fire again in 1.3 seconds; the bolt action won't lift the bullet for the trigger finger to align and fire in that time. That Mannlicher-Carcano rifle was twenty-five years old; Oswald paid £4. 5s. for it by mail-order. The ammunition for it was no less old...

A forty-five-year-old steamfitter, Howard Brennan, was the only witness to identify Lee Harvey Oswald as the man who fired the rifle. He was across the street from the Book Depository. He was a hundred feet from the building wall, and about 120 feet from the southeast corner window of the sixth floor. Brennan swore the man was standing up and firing. To fire from that window, sixty feet up on the sixth floor, one must either kneel or lie; the lattice window slides up only at the bottom. If Oswald fired that gun from that window, which was sixty feet from the ground, he was hitting a slow-moving target, with a sight attachment, at 260 feet with a twenty-seven degree angle. For this feat the Warren Commission allows him seven seconds.

After the shooting at 12.33 that morning, Oswald, it is claimed, was stopped by an officer[1] for a moment, in the canteen inside the building; the officer was told he was an employee, the officer ran on. Oswald left the building, walked seven blocks on Elm Street where the firing had been, took a bus which turned back towards Elm Street, got out of the bus, walked several more blocks, took a taxi ride, walked more blocks to his room, where he stayed a couple of minutes to change, hurriedly left, waited at a bus stop, then walked almost a mile to Patton Avenue. There, he himself approached a police car, leant inside, stepped away and turned and gunned down the Officer J. D. Tippit who suddenly leapt out of the car. All in forty-three minutes. Tippit was killed at 1.15.

[*The film of Oswald's brief press conference comes on the screen. The hurried voices, the shoutings.*]

If Oswald had been tried in a court of law, he would have been presented with the evidence of his palm-print on a gun he undoubtedly owned; he certainly would have been charged with the murder of Officer Tippit; and the witness to him shooting from the Book Depository building, and the other witness to him killing Tippit . . . but his wife Marina could never have testified against him as she has done. Howard Brennan, who claims he saw Oswald fire from a sixth-floor window at the motorcade, and Helen Markham[2] who

1. Marrion L. Baker.
2. *Vide* testimonies of Benavides, Clemons, Scoggins, Higgins, Davis, Calloway and Reynolds.

says she saw Oswald shoot down Tippit – their reliability is in question; what they might say in court is not absolutely watertight. There are great grave masses of mystery the Warren Commission have not cleared up. Lee Harvey Oswald spent forty-eight hours in the Dallas police station until at 11.21 a.m. he was gunned down by Jack Ruby with a single shot. Oswald was being transferred to the County jail.

[*The film of Ruby approaching Oswald in the basement of the station; Ruby firing his gun. Oswald collapsing.*]

There are strange stories. There is circumstantial evidence about Ruby himself, and his involvement in Cuban activities.[1] Nobody can really explain why, fifteen minutes after the shooting of the President, such an intense witch-hunt of Oswald took place.[2] Nor can anyone, least of all the Warren Commission, explain why John F. Kennedy was gunned down that day. The more years that pass, the more rumours. The speculation becomes myth, and the myth presents a parody of reality.

What is irrefutable is the speed with which the first two bullets were fired.[3]

What is indelible in our minds is that the President's head received a fatal strike from the last bullet – which was either the third or the fourth shot.

Three doctors, on that fatal Friday, announced at their press conference that the wound on the President's neck had the appearance of an entry wound.[4]

1. *Hearings*, xiv, pp. 330–64. Testimony of Nancy Perrin Rich.
2. A description of the suspect in the assassination matching Oswald's description, was broadcast by the Dallas police just before 12.45 p.m. on 22 November.
3. Warren Commission Report, p. 106.
4. Dr Malcolm Perry, Dr Kemp Clark. *New York Times*, 23 November 1963. Dr Charles Carrico. *Hearings*, xviii, p. 2.

Later, after the F.B.I. pressed them to reconsider their verdict, the doctors at Parkland Memorial Hospital reversed their judgement.

It is not possible to know who has seen the photographs of the wounds or the X-ray pictures.

If Lee Harvey Oswald did it, he could not have done it alone. If he did not, he must be the hit[1] of the century. If he was involved, and somehow double-crossed, alive today must be persons with the guilt of awful silence.

1. Stool pigeon.

ACT ONE

The stage is dark. Three figures stand in the foreground. A voice speaks from the audience. MARINA *is lit.*

COMMISSION: Mrs Oswald you be at your ease, and the interpreter will tell you what I ask and you take your time about your answers. Will you state your name please?

MARINA: Marina, my name is Marina Nikolaevna Oswald. My maiden name was Prusakova.

COMMISSION: Where do you live Mrs Oswald?

MARINA: At the present time I live in Dallas ...

COMMISSION: Mrs Oswald do you have a family?

MARINA: I have two children, two girls, June will be two years old in February, and Rachel is three months old.

COMMISSION: Are you the widow of the late Lee Harvey Oswald?

MARINA: Yes ...

COMMISSION: Do you recall the date that you arrived in the United States with your husband Lee Harvey Oswald?

MARINA: On the 13th of June 1962. I am not quite certain as to the year – 61 or 62 I think 62.

COMMISSION: How did you come to this country?

MARINA: From Moscow via Poland, Germany and Holland, we came to Amsterdam by train. And from Amsterdam to New York by ship, and New York to Dallas by air.

COMMISSION: Do you recall the name of the ship on which you came?

MARINA: I think it was the s.s. Rotterdam but I am not sure.

COMMISSION: What time of the day did you arrive in New York?

MARINA: It was about noon – or 1 p.m. – thereabouts. It is hard to remember the exact time.

COMMISSION: How long did you stay in New York at that time?

MARINA: We stayed that evening and the next twenty-four hours in a hotel in New York. And then we left the following day by air.

COMMISSION: Did you know whether or not you or your husband received any financial assistance for the trip to Texas? At that time?

MARINA: I don't know exactly where Lee got the money, but he said that his brother Robert had given him the money. But the money for the trip from the Soviet Union to New York was given to us by the American Embassy in Moscow.

COMMISSION: Do you recall what time of the day you left on the flight to Texas?

MARINA: I think that by about 5 p.m. we were already in Texas.

COMMISSION: Did you go to Dallas or Fort Worth at that time?

MARINA: In Dallas we were met by the brother, Robert, he lived in Fort Worth, and he took us from Dallas to Fort Worth and we stopped at the house.

COMMISSION: Who else stayed at Robert's house at that time besides your family?

MARINA: His family and no one else.

COMMISSION: What did his family consist of at that time?

MARINA: He and his wife, and two children a boy and a girl.

COMMISSION: How long did you stay at Robert's?

MARINA: About one to one and a half months perhaps longer, but no longer than two months.

COMMISSION: Were your relations and your husband's with Robert pleasant at that time?

MARINA: Yes they were very good. His brother's relationship to us was very good.

COMMISSION: Would you briefly describe what you did during that time when you were at Robert's?

MARINA: The first time we got there we were, of course, resting for about a week, and I was busy, of course, with my little girl who was then very little. And in my free time, of course, I helped in the household.

COMMISSION: Did your husband do anything around the house or did he seek work right away?

MARINA: For about a week he was merely talking and took a trip to the library. That is it.

COMMISSION: Then did he seek work in Fort Worth?

MARINA: Yes.

COMMISSION: And when did he find his first job there?

MARINA: While we were with Robert. It seems it was at the end of the second month that Lee found work. But at this time I don't remember the date exactly, but his mother who lived in Fort Worth at that time rented a room and she proposed that we spend some time with her, that we live with her for some time.

COMMISSION: Did you discuss with your husband this proposal of your mother-in-law to have you live with her?

MARINA: Well, she made the proposal to my husband, not to me. Of course I found out about it.

COMMISSION: Did you and he have any discussion about it after you found out about it?

MARINA: Yes, of course.

COMMISSION: You recall that discussion?

MARINA: No. I only remember the fact.

COMMISSION: Did he find work after you left Robert's then?

MARINA: Yes.

COMMISSION: You did move to be with your mother-in-law, lived with her for a time?

MARINA: Yes about three weeks. And then after three weeks Lee did not want to live with her any more and he rented an apartment.

COMMISSION: Did you know the reason why he did not want to live there any more?

MARINA: It seemed peculiar to me and didn't want to believe it but he did not love his mother, she was not quite a normal woman. Now I know this for sure.

COMMISSION: Did he tell you that at the time?

MARINA: He talked about it but since he ... [*She steps away into the darkness.*]

[*The light comes up.* MARGUERITE *and* LEE *are talking.* MARINA *joins them quite naturally as if she has been in the room with them all the time.* LEE *takes a chair and sits down as if he is tired.*]

MARGUERITE: ... I didn't even ask when you went out I didn't even ask – did I ask? If you want to go right down along there and try I'd say baby you try my honey – who would step up and argue when a clean-limbed young intelligent American steps off of this boat and all from Moscow – and all he has he can get is thirty dollars a week – I know that's criminal – but I don't stand up and say you deserve better boy – I leave that unto you –

MARINA: What is she saying?

MARGUERITE: Tried mind you – well I did – and that long trip out to Washington knowing all on you all alone in that foreign country – I'd still call it foreign you married or none to Marina – I went up to complain that they weren't hurrying enough that their fingers weren't none out not one bit – that – that I said to them.

MARINA: Oh Lee – will you please tell me –

MARGUERITE: Time to bring you back on home and forget. Won't they let a young man forget?

MARINA: Lee – you won't hear me – now what is she telling you to – do – is she angry with me? What does she shout Lee?

MARGUERITE: Even if I found you a room – it's only a room – and I take it from the man – it has loving all in it – for you to do with you what you want –

LEE: Mamma says I owe –

MARINA: Go on –

MARGUERITE: Time passes on like the bible and some say the love that one has had passes well I am old and I am young because I see in me the time stays – now –

LEE: She helped us from Russia she says –

MARINA: We can pay it back –

LEE: Sacrificed jobs and all she say.

MARINA: But speak to her.

LEE: I cannot.

MARINA: Isn't all this hers isn't it true?

LEE: Not true enough – don't ask me what's not true ...

MARGUERITE: And practise your Russian – well practise it – but I'm practising the love of a mother not practising practising – so I expect –

LEE: Not nothing do you!

MARGUERITE: Don't shout me down –

LEE: I'm sorry –

MARINA: Are you shouting at Mamma Lee?

LEE [*at the top of his voice*]: No! Not! Shouting!

MARGUERITE: When I talk with you you won't talk – when you talk to Marina I can't understand – and you won't say what you say – what is it Lee? I should die? And my broken heart and I?

LEE: Never could Mamma.

MARGUERITE: Yes ... there was a time?

LEE: Not loving Mamma.

MARGUERITE: Plenty of nights lie in my arms and you say whatever you thought the world outside had done – and there was peace I gave you peace.

LEE: I shared a bed with you Mamma until I was ten – I never could cry – could I ever say could I what I said – most times I disliked the schools and places because I never could say what it was so how could I say to you in bed – I never learnt to cry remember that? Not me. So what tears Mamma?

MARGUERITE: I saw tears ...

LEE: No Mamma ... we're going on.

MARGUERITE: Isn't it cheap enough – is it a dollar overmuch?

LEE: Mamma we don't live together – I have Marina –

MARGUERITE: You need me.

LEE: I have Marina.

[*The stage darkens again.* MARGUERITE's *voice can be heard. She walks to the front of the stage. But it is still dark.*]

MARGUERITE'S VOICE: ... and also stating that my son wishes to return back to the United States – just eight weeks after my trip to Washington.

[*We can see her clearly now. A spot lights her body. She is addressing the audience.*]

MARGUERITE: Now, you want to know why I think my son is an agent. And I have been telling you all along. Here is a very important thing why my son was an agent. On 22 March I receive a letter of his address and stating that my son wishes to return back to the United States. You have that sir?

COMMISSION: Yes.

MARGUERITE: On 30 April 1961, he marries a Russian girl – approximately five weeks later. Now why does a man who wants to come back to the United States, five weeks later – here is the proof: 30 April 1961, is the wedding date – marry a Russian girl? Because I say – and I may be wrong – the U.S. Embassy has ordered him to marry this Russian girl. And a few weeks later, 16 May 1961, he is coming home with the Russian girl. And as we know, he does get out of the Soviet Union with the Russian girl, with money loaned to him by the U.S. Embassy. I may be wrong gentlemen, but two and two in my book makes four.

COMMISSION: Mrs Oswald – you saw your daughter-in-law and your son living together with you, didn't you, for some time?

MARGUERITE: Yes, they lived with me one month.

COMMISSION: Did you think they were in love with each other?

MARGUERITE: Yes they were definitely in love with each other. Yes I think they were in love with each other.

COMMISSION: What about books? Did he read books much while he was living with you?

MARGUERITE: Yes he read continuously. He went immediately to the library upon coming to the United States. He read continuously. All kinds of books.

COMMISSION: Now was there any time that Marina said anything to you to lead you to believe that she thought your son, Lee, married her because he was an agent?

MARGUERITE: No Sir no Sir not at any time at all.

COMMISSION: You think she loved him?

MARGUERITE: I believe that Marina loved him in a way. But I believe that Marina wanted to come to America. I believe that Lee had talked American to her, and she wanted to come to America. Maybe she loved him. I am sure she did anyway. She said that she did.

COMMISSION: I am not clear about this being ordered to marry her. You don't mean that your son didn't love her?

MARGUERITE: Well I could mean that – if he is an agent, and he has a girlfriend, and it is to the benefit of the country that he marry this girlfriend, and the Embassy helped him to get this Russian girl out of Russia, let's face it, whether he loved her or not, he would take her to America, if that would give him contact with Russians, yes, sir.

COMMISSION: Is that what you mean?

MARGUERITE: I would say that.

COMMISSION: How did you get along when you were there together with Marina and your son?

MARGUERITE: Well that was a very happy month. Marina was very happy. She had the best home I believe that she had ever had ... [*The stage lights up again. She walks back to* LEE *who is where he was in the earlier scene* MARINA *described.*] ... I didn't even ask you when you went out I didn't even ask – did I ask? If you want to go right down along there and try I'd say baby you try my honey.

MARINA: Lee please –

LEE: I can't get no job – I got to get work –

MARGUERITE: But that's why you go down at the library – and you learn –

LEE: You don't see – I'm married – not in a cot now –

MARGUERITE: Are you married? I mean you suddenly got yourself a wife and a child – but do I come in there – I mean where do I come in there – I mean where do I come in – I'm saying nobody forgets a mother –

LEE: I know that Mamma – but Marina must eat – so must I – and June too – I ain't living off you none –

MARGUERITE: Did you ever?

LEE: I tried hard – you ask Robert – he knows – we all know we never wanted to live off of you – now did we?

MARGUERITE: Time was –

LEE: That's sentiment Mamma. Time is. I learn something a little bit everywhere – there's more'n in this world to hate than there is to like –

MARINA: Lee – say to me what she says?

LEE: I say nobody's happy –

MARINA: Lee say to me you love me?

LEE: Oh yes.

MARGUERITE: God knows I've been good.

LEE: What does that mean?

MARGUERITE: You and I have loved – and Robert too – in New York remember?

LEE: But I ran away far enough –

MARGUERITE: From the government from the system – oh I know there's a system you hate –

LEE: It's just – I mean just possibly it is the thing I hate which you can't really hate –

MARGUERITE: You love me Lee –

LEE: That's what I hate Mamma.

MARGUERITE: No . . .

LEE: And we go on talking love and fellow man – and there's Washington and Lincoln who are dead, and Marx is dead, and we feebly talk on love – what does it – it makes the world go on round?

MARGUERITE: I'm bitterly upset –

LEE: No.

MARGUERITE: You force me out – now if I go out and get something nice even if it's for Marina here who doesn't hear me when I say –

LEE: You cain't afford it –

MARGUERITE: Afford love?

LEE: I didn't say that –

MARGUERITE: Nevertheless ... [*She puts on a coat and walks away.*]

[*LEE tries to follow her.*]

LEE: It's not gifts – and – and – it's not love –

MARGUERITE: You say right on – one more word – you forcing me on like this.

[*LEE stands haplessly. He watches her go.*]

MARINA: Lee please?

LEE: She feels guilt –

MARINA: I sat here and listened – and you both don't speak to me –

LEE: Darling – she never does anything – Mamma likes to talk because she feels all the time – and she has never done life – she feels it – I do it –

MARINA: I'd like –

LEE: I feel I'm losing my hair that it's falling out – that's a feeling – but I'm not standing up in Congress and say all that for it – you stand up and say world you say world and democracies – and wrongs – oh there are wrongs.

MARINA: I'd like the television box on please Lee –

LEE: And when you got democracies you have here

votes which none use properly – you say what? What?

MARINA: Gregory Peck.

LEE: Honey I'm not counting with you –

MARINA: Mamma said there was Gregory Peck this afternoon – could I see him. We have him – he was showing in Minsk remember –

LEE: No you cannot.

MARINA: I need to learn –

LEE: There's my way. Don't need no commercial slick hogwash – about Hollywood? Oh come on now . . . !

MARINA: June is sleeping.

LEE: Let me tell you – Gregory Peck will as certain as the red sun make June holler now – and all night.

MARINA: Then I do nothing.

LEE: No you don't.

MARINA: There'll be no washed dishes and Mamma will call you out for that –

LEE: You sit down.

MARINA: I'm sitting down –

LEE: Now I'll sit here –

MARINA: Did you love that other girl in Minsk – the girl in your diary – love her more than –

LEE: I won't discuss love!

MARINA: Ordinary people need to –

LEE: I am not ordinary. I'll discuss books, politics and great men – because that's all we ever learn from – I'm giving you learning now – will you watch?

MARINA: No. I want Gregory Peck.

LEE: What is that?

MARINA: I'm not blind.

LEE: I'm holding it up – now what is that?

MARINA: Ormin.

LEE: What do you mean 'ormin'.

MARINA: Orm.

LEE: *This* is my orm – I mean 'arm', not orm nothing
Marina – but I'm holding up this –

[MARINA *'climbs' up his arm and kisses the fingers on his hand.*]

Say – hand?

MARINA: Haarrnd.

LEE: It's hand.

MARINA: Aarnd.

LEE: Marina – what would you say if I said my harrnd
ais oown moi ormin?

MARINA: That's very good – ten out of ten! [*She laughs.*]

[LEE *sits humoured but saddened, shakes his head.*]

LEE: In English – what do you write on – or – no – what
do you read?

MARINA: Book?

LEE: Very good. And when I nod my head what do we
mean –

MARINA: Yes Mamma.

LEE: No Mamma!

MARINA: No Mamma.

LEE: When I go up and down like this?

MARINA: Yes Mamma.

[*The lights dim a little.* LEE *and* MARINA *continue
talking. Their voices fade.*]

[*A spot picks out* MARGUERITE *who faces the audience.
She holds in her hand a child's highchair. The rest of the
stage is dark.*]

MARGUERITE: And of course Marina and Lee spoke
Russian all the time even in front of me. And you
asked me about this time – it was a happy time. They
would sit at the table, they were playing a game, and I
said to Lee what is it you are doing? Because they were
always talking in Russian. Mother – we are playing a
game which is similar to American tic-tac-toe. And

they also taught each other. They had books. They are both children – very intelligent and studious. Lee was teaching Marina English, and Marina was teaching him some things that he wanted to know about Russia, in my home. [*The lights come up. She walks around the stage. She comes in again where she left them both before.*]

[LEE *is still teaching* MARINA.]

LEE: There is in this room – what is there Marina?

MARINA [*points out objects slowly*]: ... table ... book ... chair ... Lee ... television box.

[MARGUERITE *bustles in.*]

... Mamma!

MARGUERITE: Give that to her – tell her Lee –

LEE: No I refuse to.

MARGUERITE: Then I'll do it myself.

LEE: You do these things because you're guilty or something –

[MARGUERITE *hands the highchair to* MARINA *gently.* MARINA *is confused.*]

MARINA: How do I say thank you Lee? Is it for me Lee?

LEE: You say no thanks. Hear me?

MARINA: No thanks Mamma.

MARGUERITE: I don't understand –

MARINA: Lee – tell me what it is? I don't sit in it do I?

LEE: I want you to understand right here and now – to stop giving me and Marina gifts – can you afford them? No Sir you can't. I'll give her what is necessary, the best I can do.

MARGUERITE: I was trying Lee –

MARINA: Is it for the baby? I've never seen a thing like that –

LEE: Hear what she says – I'll translate – she don't even know what it is for! Listen to me – because today or tomorrow you take sick and you spend all your money on us – I will have to take care of you. Now come on Mamma I ain't going to take care of you when I've got thirty dollars a week am I? Fact is too – I don't have thirty dollars a week right now –

MARGUERITE: We'll go out – right now – we'll find a job – you and I – there's this woman at the Texas employment agency – don't you recall how she was ever calling you on up – and say I got this job and that job?

LEE: But Marina –

MARGUERITE: We won't be long. I'll help you find a job – right now – right now you see –

LEE: Mamma I'll find a job – my way –

MARGUERITE: You'll find one – with me – and we'll buy cakes – but right now with me – in my car.

LEE: Why do I always go? I was stronger about you when I was a kid – I'd say go to hell Mamma – and don't come back any . . .

MARGUERITE: I'm waiting . . . [*She taps her foot.*]

[LEE *suddenly seems cowed. He doesn't want to go. But he does. He pulls a short jerkin from a chair. Slowly so slowly he puts it on.*]

LEE: Marina . . . [*He kisses her briefly. She looks up at him.*] We won't be gone long. . . .

[*They both leave. A door slams shut somewhere.* MARINA *picks up a large rag doll and sits it in front of the highchair. She faces the highchair towards the television set. She switches the set on. The sound comes on. It is the Gregory Peck movie. June in the next room begins to cry. She cries some more.* MARINA *goes over to a table, pulls out a packet of cigarettes from under the table. They are glued under the table with chewing gum. She unsticks the gum, and takes out a cigarette. June cries louder.* MARINA *increases the*

38

sound from the movie. She sits back and watches the noisy television.]

[*Darkness again. Fade Out*]

[*The stage is dark.* MARINA *walks to the front of the stage. A spot picks up her face. The voice from the audience carries on as if there has been no interruption.*]

COMMISSION: When you moved to Dallas where did you live the first time?

MARINA: I did not move to Dallas together with Lee. Lee went to Dallas when he found the job, and I remained in Fort Worth and lived with Elena Hall.

COMMISSION: For how long a period did you live with Mrs Hall?

MARINA: I think that it was about a month and a half.

COMMISSION: During that month and a half what did your husband do?

MARINA: He had a job. He was working. He would call me up over the telephone but how he spent his time, I don't know.

COMMISSION: Do you know during that month and a half where he lived?

MARINA: At first I know that he rented a room in the Y.M.C.A. but very shortly thereafter he rented an apartment. But where I don't know.

COMMISSION: During that month and a half did he come to see you and the baby?

MARINA: Yes two or three times he came to see us because he had no car. It was not very easy.

COMMISSION: After this month and a half did he find a place for you all to live together?

MARINA: Yes but it wasn't a problem there to find a place, no problem there to find a place.

COMMISSION: Did you then move to a home in Dallas?

MARINA: Yes, on Elsbeth Street in Dallas.

COMMISSION: Did you observe any guns in your things when you moved?

MARINA: No.

COMMISSION: Did you have a telephone there?

MARINA: No.

COMMISSION: What about his reading habits there — were they the same?

MARINA: Yes about the same.

COMMISSION: Can you tell us a little more fully about his reading? Did he spend several hours each evening in this reading?

MARINA: Yes.

COMMISSION: Do you recall any of the books that he read at Elsbeth Street?

MARINA: No. He had two books, two thick books on the history of the United States.

COMMISSION: Did you go out in the evenings?

MARINA: Yes.

COMMISSION: Where did you go?

MARINA: Sometimes we went shopping to stores, and movies, though Lee really went to the movies himself. He wanted to take me but I did not understand English. Then on weekends he would go to a lake not far away or to a park or to the cafe for some ice-cream.

COMMISSION: Were either you or your husband taking any schooling at that time?

MARINA: Lee took English courses or typing courses ...

COMMISSION: About what time would he get home from work?

MARINA: About 5 to 5.30.

COMMISSION: Then would you eat your evening meal?

MARINA: Yes.

COMMISSION: How soon after that would he leave for the class?

MARINA: When Lee took his courses he generally did not come home for dinner, usually he didn't.

COMMISSION: Did he practise his typewriting at home at all?

MARINA: At home no. But he had a book, a textbook on typing which he would review when he was at home.

COMMISSION: How soon after the class was over did he come home ordinarily?

MARINA: Nine o'clock.

COMMISSION: Did he tell you anything about friends that he met at these classes?

MARINA: No.

COMMISSION: While you were at Elsbeth Street do you recall seeing any guns in your apartment?

MARINA: No.

COMMISSION: When did you move to Neely Street from the Elsbeth Street apartment?

MARINA: In January after the New Year. I don't remember exactly.

COMMISSION: Do you remember why you moved from Elsbeth Street to Neely Street?

MARINA: I like it better on Neely Street. We had a porch there. And that was more convenient for the child.

COMMISSION: Did you have any differences with your husband while you were at Neely Street?

MARINA: No. Well there are always some reasons for some quarrel between a husband and wife, not everything is always smooth.

COMMISSION: I had in mind if there was any violence or any hitting of you. Did that occur at Neely Street?

MARINA: No. That was on Elsbeth Street.

COMMISSION: Do you recall what brought that about?

MARINA: Not quite. I am trying to remember. It seems to me that it was at that time that Lee began to talk

about his wanting to return to Russia. I did not want
that and that is why we had quarrels.

COMMISSION: Did you have discussions between you
about this idea of returning to Russia?

MARINA: Yes. Lee wanted me to ... [*She steps back into
the stage.*]

   [*The lights rise up.* LEE *is in the room with her on Elsbeth
   Street. There is a cot near the wall, beside an open
   window. He is talking agitatedly.*]

LEE: ... I've been considering – Marina – now I've been
considering –

MARINA: You say that twice –

LEE: What I said before when I said –

MARINA: Only say I said –

LEE: My Russian isn't good!

MARINA: Shout!

LEE: I ain't – I'm breathing – don't you see – you needle
me some.

MARINA: Do I? What about Lee – dear Lee –

LEE: Oh come on! You know I hate that sort of stuff –

MARINA: Then – I was only joking. I wasn't making a
pass at you –

LEE: That's what I mean Marina.

MARINA: It's very difficult to know what you ever
mean –

LEE: I mean if you're loving sometimes it was a joke and
if you are not loving it still is – and I don't know you.
I don't. We're not here – you talk in Russian with me
Marina like this and all – isn't it a game? A sort of way
of living? Not – living.

MARINA: I don't understand you Lee.

LEE: As I was saying before I got interrupted – I was
saying what I mean – I was saying.

MARINA: You said –

LEE: Will you listen! Once in my life – will you let me – I'll tell it and well Marina I'll say it all well in good Russian if you'll stop – there now. [*They stare at each other. He finds it difficult to say what comes into his mind because he forgets words easily.*] You stop? For Lee?

MARINA: I stop you stop he stop –

LEE: I want you to go on back . . . it all can't be the same as it was . . . I remember snow and the cold, things like lines for potatoes because the crop stay down in the earth and no one no matter how he try get it up out of the grass . . . that was Minsk Marina.

MARINA: I forget it –

LEE: Sure you do. But that's as how it was. This is no place here now what is all this if it ain't another kind of poverty – it's warm, fruit is cheap –

MARINA: Then you like it.

LEE: It's a desert. Nothing nurtures. There is no reality you don't feel the rest of the world and all its problems come crowding in on this room here –

MARINA: Do I have to Lee?

LEE: Texas thinks only about Texas. Ask a Texan where all those Russkies come from he don't know – he'll tell you they come from off of the moon or something like and they going hit us with red flying saucers from up there – hey!

MARINA: Yes Lee.

LEE: No Lee! . . . Marina, you go back . . .

MARINA: And line for potatoes – are you mad – I sometime wonder if I am not understanding the language – but you are!

LEE: It would be better –

MARINA: Make sense Lee! If you send me away you don't love me.

LEE: I do of course but –

43

MARINA: You lie.

LEE: No Marina.

MARINA: And I not come back? Have I a chance to ever come back again?

LEE: I'll join you – but later – I must have time –

MARINA: How do I know that?

LEE: You don't. Trust.

MARINA: After we have come ten thousand miles – how can I possibly ever go back? If you want me to go – you never loved right from the start. I did.

LEE: Perhaps we have both forgot the loving – if it was there anyway. But you're going back to Russia. I say you are.

MARINA: Give me one good reason?

LEE: It just would be better that way.

MARINA: What would – what in the name of God would!

LEE: We mustn't shout – the baby.

MARINA: I'll shout.

[LEE *hits her in the mouth with a half-closed fist.* MARINA *grabs his arm and tries to kick back at him.*]

LEE: No.

MARINA: And I'm a woman too!

LEE: I want you to go on home –

MARINA: I won't – you see I defeat you – I stay silent I say nothing. I won't talk about it. It is forgotten – wiped off. I say nothing. You hit me you see – I say nothing.

[LEE *hits her again in the chest.* MARINA *grips her breast. She is hurt. She won't shout.*]

LEE: Nothing works Marina – not ever – now you'll go – won't you ? [*He hits her. She falls back on the bed. She refuses to speak.*] You'll say you will – or I'll do it again – [*She shakes her head furiously.*]

You'll say it and you'll say it – and you'll go back

home! [*He hits her on her face, on her neck, on her shoulders. She holds her hand to her mouth to stop her screaming.*] Let the child wake up – you both go –

[MARINA *stuffs a piece of the cotton bedspread into her mouth so that she cannot scream.*

LEE *stops hitting her. She shakes a little. She lies where she falls on the bed.* LEE *sits in a corner crosslegged in the room. He stares at her.*]

... you know Marina ... I don't think you ever loved me at all ... I didn't believe you when you said it in Minsk – I mean I was already in love with somebody else Marina – you came along – but isn't it just possible between you and me neither of us had much love – you call it love, Mamma calls it love – but it's a way of jealousy and possession and I can't abide none of that now ... If you only did what I said once – were not so lazy – if you once played ball – I'd come back to you – wherever you are. In New York when I was at junior high they began to call me Ossie Rabbit – now they said Ossie was for Oswald, and I kept popping up in strange places so that when they saw me peep over a wall to see the gang there – they'd say there goes Ossie Rabbit. I remember ... Marina you're not listening any ... Marina ... now Marina what if that baby ups and starts ...

[*We dim the stage again. His voice fades. It is black once more.*]

[*From the gloom* MARGUERITE *steps forward. It is obvious she has been talking for some time. She appears to be in mid paragraph.*]

MARGUERITE: ... It has been stated in the paper that my son was giving Marina black eyes and possibly had beat her. And this is by the Russian people. Now living in this home in Fort Worth, I had gone by several times I had a day off, and Marina was not at home. I said to her Marina, Mamma come to see you yesterday. You no home. She didn't answer. I said Marina Mamma come see you. You no home. Marina. No. I go to lady's house to take English lessons.

COMMISSION: Do you know who she was speaking of?

MARGUERITE: I do not know for a fact. But my son Robert will know. And that is why it is important to call him. That is what I am trying to say Chief Justice Warren. These others will know this part of my story, give you the facts. I am assuming it is Mr Peter Gregory's wife that started these lessons. But Marina was taking English lessons. Now, they lived at a corner house, and there is Carol Street, and opposite Carol Street is a parking lot for Montgomery Ward. They live approximately two blocks from Montgomery Ward. So I had gone by, as I am stating, several times. You have to understand – this is just six or seven weeks that they are in this home.

COMMISSION: You say 'they'. I am sorry to interrupt.

MARGUERITE: Marina and Lee in this home ... Then Marina was not home. I could not understand where so fast that they could have so many friends, that this Russian girl didn't speak English and know her way about, could be gone all day long. That worried me. So I sat in the car on Montgomery Ward's parking lot, where I could see the house, because I wanted to see who Marina was going to come home with. The door was open. I went in the house and no one was there. But this time, I was wondering how she could be gone all the time, being a stranger in town. I sat in the car all day long. She didn't show up. Finally I went home, had my supper, left my apartment, and on the way going back to the house Lee was leaving Montgomery Ward. He got in the car with me and we had about a block to go. I entered the home with Lee, and I said – Lee, where is Marina? Of course, I knew that she wasn't home, because I had stayed in the car all day. He said – oh I guess she is out with some friends. Would you like me to fix your supper? No. She will probably be home in time to fix my supper. And I left. I'm not going to interfere in their married life. But I did offer to fix him supper. And I went back to make sure Marina still wasn't home. I walked in the home with my son. So approximately two days later – not approximately, but two days later, I went to the home and my son was reading, he read continuously – in the living-room, and Marina was in the bedroom. I could not see Marina. And I said to Lee –

[*The lights come up again.* LEE *sits front stage.* MARINA *her back turned away is on a bed back stage. There is a strained silence.* MARGUERITE *stares at* LEE *uncertainly.*]

MARGUERITE: Lee then?

LEE: Yes Mamma?

MARGUERITE: You could smile some –

LEE: Say what you want Mamma.

MARGUERITE: You don't want to talk?

LEE: Been talking – just right now.

MARGUERITE: What kind of?

LEE: Just talk.

MARGUERITE: Politics?

LEE: No sir.

MARGUERITE: Philosophics?

LEE: Now no.

MARGUERITE: There's only one thing you two ever can sit down and talk about.

LEE: We are not quarrelling Mamma.

MARGUERITE: It's very silent – like an icebox.

LEE: Iceboxes'll hum Mamma – you know like – bbbrrrrrrhhh.

MARGUERITE: Because I'm only ever thinking of helping –

LEE: Yes.

MARGUERITE: It seems strange when I sees people not talking when God gives tongues –

LEE: No reason to talk anymore Mamma when you come in – you talk enough for three –

MARGUERITE: That I do when my mind's made up –

LEE: But the baby must have quiet see.

MARGUERITE: Is that a historical philosophic book you are reading?

LEE: Biography of George Washington.

MARGUERITE: Tell Marina I am here.

[LEE *ignores her and reads his book.* MARINA *sits like a piece of George Segal in white plaster. Turned away just that little bit.*]

Lee?

[LEE *reads. He shrinks lower in his chair.*]

Marina? [*She crosses the stage.* To MARINA:] . . . Marina baby – it's Mamma.

[MARINA *turns around. She is nursing young June. June is a white swath of cloth. She has a markedly clear black eye. She has bruises on her face.*

MARGUERITE *tries to touch* MARINA. MARINA *stands away. She genuflects back from* MARGUERITE.]

MARGUERITE: Baby – who did that?

[MARINA *doesn't understand.* MARGUERITE *points out the mark on* MARINA's *face.*]

MARINA: Mamma – Lee.

MARGUERITE: When honey?

MARINA: Mamma – Lee. [*Something doll-like and pathetic*

about MARGUERITE *this time. She is utterly bewildered, she doesn't know her surroundings or her friends.*]

[MARGUERITE *walks back up front.*]

MARGUERITE: Lee – what do you mean?

LEE: Come again?

MARGUERITE: Striking Marina?

LEE: Oh that . . .

MARGUERITE: Tell me.

LEE: Mother – that is our affair.

MARGUERITE: But I think you are a louse for it. I may know what goes on but there is no need to hit the girl.

[LEE *ignores* MARGUERITE. *He is talking to* MARINA *in Russian.* MARGUERITE *doesn't understand them.*]

LEE: Mamma says she been watching you – Marina? What do you say?

MARGUERITE: Lee – I was addressing you in English I was –

LEE: What do you say Marina?

MARINA: Mamma would.

LEE: Yearh she would – I can just see – and all – following you on down the street and saying now just why does she stay inside that house all the day?

MARINA: I told you Lee.

LEE: Sure. Mamma knows. You go see Paul Gregory for those English lessons – and it all makes sense.

MARINA: Russian lessons! He said he wanted to learn Russian –

LEE: And he's a nice good-looking all American – and he wants to further his mind – what about that? [*He turns savagely on* MARGUERITE.] . . . And when I want to broaden my mind Mamma – what do they say – he's a nut! Give him ten dollars a day, and a few straight words from the John Birch Society and he's all fixed up ready to die – what is it Mamma that makes me not want to be this year's automobile? The model, which, when you buy it, you can't even afford to sell it secondhand because the price don't cover the credit tag! What is it about America when you can't afford to live in it, and I hear – now, cost of dying is so high the Lord's fixing on his own insurance scheme! [*He turns back to* MARINA. *He is speaking in Russian.*] And who's a clean-cut all American boy! What is it I ought to give you because now you've a nice young foreign friend? An English lesson! You want an English education – that kind of education is the same language in the same bed all over the world!

MARINA: You're shouting Lee.

LEE: No I'm not. I'm just holding my mouth a little more open.

MARGUERITE: Lee – I have already spoken to Marina –

LEE: So have I –

MARGUERITE: You have hit her not –

LEE: I always thought – Marina – you came to me – like I was always here – and I thought I'd teach Marina English and Marina would show me Russian – and it would always be a fair mutual honest exchange –

MARGUERITE: Lee you're not listening to me none – now what I came to see and I wouldn't have said it unless my conscience pricked me – seeing you two fighting –

LEE: Somehow – dead or alive Mamma – the last word is always yours.

MARGUERITE: I was saying! Dammit! How is it Marina says she goes for English lessons to the young man – when his family says it is Russian lessons Marina give him – and all the day long I stand there and see too well – Marina don't come home! Explain me that?

LEE: Because Mamma – it must be, my English ain't that good enough.

MARGUERITE: For her?

[*The stage blackens. There is a pause in time.*]

[*The darkness is relieved by a spot which picks up the shape of* MARINA. *She comes forward to the audience. She seems composed. She waits until the* COMMISSIONER *puts his questions. But she has been answering his questions all day.*]

COMMISSION: Did you observe some time when you thought he changed?

MARINA: I would say that immediately after coming to the United States Lee changed. I did not know him as such a man in Russia.

COMMISSION: Will you describe how you observed these changes and what they were as you saw them?

MARINA: He helped me as before but he became a little more of a recluse. He did not like my Russian friends and he tried to forbid me to have anything to do with them. He was very irritable, sometimes for a trifle, for a trifling reason.

COMMISSION: Did he tell you why he did not like your Russian friends?

MARINA: I don't know why he didn't like them. I didn't understand. At least that which he said was completely unfounded. He simply said some stupid or foolish things.

COMMISSION: Will you tell us the stupid things that he said?

MARINA: Well, he thought that they were fools for having left Russia; they were all traitors. I would tell him he was in the same position being an American in America but there were really no reasons just irritation. He said that they all only like money, and everything is measured by money. It seems to me that perhaps he was envious of them in the sense they were more prosperous than he was. When I told him, when I would say that to him he did not like to hear that. Perhaps I shouldn't say these foolish things and I feel kind of uncomfortable to talk about the foolish things that happened or what he said foolish things. This is one of the reasons why I don't really know the reasons for these quarrels because sometimes these quarrels were just trifles. It is just that Lee was very unrestrained and very explosive at that time.

COMMISSION: Mrs Oswald, we will ask you to be very frank with us. It isn't for the purpose of embarrassing you or your husband that we ask you these things but it might help us to understand and even if you will tell us the foolish and stupid things it may shed some light on the problem. You understand that?

MARINA: I understand that you are not asking these questions out of curiosity but for a reason.

COMMISSION: Did your husband indicate any particular Russian friends that he disliked more than others?

MARINA: He liked de Mohrenschildt but he – because he was a strong person, but only de Mohrenschildt. He did not like Bouhe or Anna Meller.

COMMISSION: Did you ever tell him you liked these people?

MARINA: Yes. I told him all the time that I liked these people and that is why he was angry at me and would tell me that I was just like they were. At one time I left him and went to my friends because he put me into – put me on the spot by saying – well if you like your friends so much then go ahead and live with them. And he left me no choice.

COMMISSION: When was this Mrs Oswald?

MARINA: On Elsbeth Street.

COMMISSION: How long were you gone from him then?

MARINA: One week.

COMMISSION: Did he ask you to return?

MARINA: Yes. I took June and I went to Anna Meller, took a cab and went there. I spent several days with her. Lee didn't know where I was but he called up and about two or three days after I came to and we met at de Mohrenschildt's house and he asked me to return home. I, of course, did not want a divorce but I told him it would be better to get a divorce rather than to continue living and quarrelling this way. After all this is only a burden on a man if two people live together and fight. I simply wanted to show him too, that I am not a toy. That a woman is a little more complicated. That you cannot trifle with her.

COMMISSION: Did you say anything at that time about how he should treat you if you returned?

MARINA: Yes. I told him if he did not change his character, then it would become impossible to continue living with him. Because if there should be such quarrels continuously that would be crippling for the children.

COMMISSION: What did he say to that?

MARINA: Then he said that it would be – it was very hard for him. That he could not change. That I must accept him, such as he was. And he asked me to come back home with him right on that day but he left feeling bad because I did not go and remained with my friend.

COMMISSION: Then did he get in touch with you again?

MARINA: At that time there was very little room at Anna Meller's and it was very uncomfortable and I left and went to Katya Ford whose husband at that time happened to be out of town on business. I spent several days with Katya Ford but then when her husband returned I did not want to remain with her. And it was on a Sunday morning then when I moved over to Anna Ray. Lee called me and said he wanted to see me and he came that evening ...

[*The lights come up.* MARINA *walks back into the stage.* LEE *is looking curiously around. They talk in Russian.* MARINA *is artificially calm.* LEE *is troubled but sort of witty about things.*]

LEE: Which hotel is this?

MARINA: She is a kind of friend of mine she let me stay –

LEE: So was Katya.

MARINA: Yes.

LEE: So was Anna Meller.

MARINA: But I chose to come here.

LEE: Throw you out did they?

MARINA: I chose to.

LEE: Run out of friends soon Marina.

MARINA: You already have. Who do I have to turn to – I must make my own.

LEE: Funny how they're not mine – not a manjack there is a friend of mine –

MARINA: They are married women – who have families – they also have ... [*She won't say. She cuts her tongue off.*]

LEE: Have what?

MARINA: I was going to say – husbands.

LEE: You mean like a lover not a husband –

MARINA: He should be both!

LEE: This one ain't.

MARINA: There was a time –

LEE: Now why do women always go back – into the past – there was there was – but I'm here now honey.

MARINA: I'm not hungry. You can have what's on my plate –

LEE: Like it's a dog what crawls in – and you feed it?

MARINA: Just sit down – be calm – if you don't want it –

LEE: I do. [*He sits at the table.* MARINA *fetches him some bread.*] ... Nice place. Does she pay the rent and all? Or –

MARINA: She's a nice woman –

LEE: Yearh? Where do you sleep?

MARINA: That's a funny question.

LEE: I don't ever ask you where you sleep do I?

MARINA: No.

LEE: As if I don't really want to know?

MARINA: Yes.

LEE: I do. I really do. It's interesting. It's always fine and satisfactory to know just where your wife is sleeping case comes a bad night and you ain't got no bunk yourself – says I. [MARINA *stands smiling at him. He eats only a little.*] I'd like to see sleeping – that's a waste of time – and eating – do you realize three meals a day, half an hour at breakfast, an hour and a half at luncheon and two hours in the evening time – what is that?

MARINA: I can't count that far.

LEE: I can – you rely on Decimals Lee you're one straight goodies man – that is – eh, four hours daily and it's got to go – now in four hours you could have written a sonnet, launched an I C B M or –

MARINA: Become a better man?

[LEE *sits and stares and thinks. It takes time. He decides he doesn't like it any. It's a crack.*]

LEE: Cut that out. Who's been talking at you?

MARINA: Nobody, Lee.

LEE: All that you can cut out –

MARINA: I'm sorry –

LEE: There's no butter!

MARINA: I'll get some –

LEE: That's not the point – what for do you bring bread and then there is no butter to go on the bread. This ain't no Minsk is it now!

MARINA: Lee I forgot –

LEE: It's that it's only Lee – that half shot-off husband come to bore all you all to all hell death – give Ossie Rabbit the bones!

MARINA: You're being impossible –

LEE: I'm saying it's symbolic. Where's the butter Marina – where's the cream on the top of the milk that old great society milk fed – what do you want a new car?

MARINA: I don't want anything that I have to ask for.

LEE: Oldsmobile?

MARINA: The joke is over –

LEE: Not a Ford – not a showy Caddie – you want a Stingray – you want a Corvette –

[MARINA *goes into the kitchen. She comes back with a plate of butter.* LEE *is still provoking. She places it on the table in front of him.*]

Then in great American hardware stores – you find a plastic foodmix, or a chromium icebox or a record-player or even buy a long-playing record of music 'for people who don't want to waste their time listening to music anyway'! How about that – [*He sees the butter. He throws it across the floor.*]

MARINA: I just brought you it Lee!

LEE: Lee's changed his mind.

MARINA: Lee – you're insane!

LEE: Don't ever say that – I see clear as sunlight I see I do!

MARINA: You asked for butter –

LEE: Now I don't want it!

MARINA: ... what is it? What can I do? I have never known by night or day – what it is you want? ...

[LEE *is stopped at that sad sound in her voice.*]

LEE: A way.

MARINA: Where?

LEE: To understand.

MARINA: Understand what?

LEE: A way to understand ... that's all.

[MARINA *scoops up the butter carefully. He is on his knees helping her.*]

MARINA: You're not helping me Lee – you keep putting your knees in the butter while I –

LEE: I want you back home –

MARINA: No.

LEE: Yes. It's gonna be. It doesn't work any other way –

MARINA: Not for all the shouting –

LEE: I'm like that. Aren't I? I don't breathe right when you're gone –

MARINA: You have no one to shout at?

LEE: I can't – I won't want to live anymore than now – if you don't. I don't have anything else. Sure I loathe it. I haven't the collateral the way to live with money – I don't even know where money is – what it looks like – I boasted about America in Minsk – now I'm ashamed I don't give you America – America is two rooms and a cold-water place and I'm sorry – if it were different you'd be happier oh I know ...

MARINA: You really want me to go back –

LEE: Home.

MARINA: No. You really mean I go back to Russia –

LEE: I mean to Neely Street with me –

MARINA: No. Say what you first said. I must go home.

What you said remember – Marina go back to Russia
I'll feel better you can get work there and I'll join you –

LEE: I don't mean that –

MARINA: You only say what you partially mean you
only do what you need to do Lee – say it all do it all in
one.

LEE: Marina I have nothing I am nothing – I am awfully
alone. I won't talk about Russia – just accept I am as
you see me. Will you come on home? And bring June?

MARINA: Not for a while ...

LEE: I won't shout none ...

MARINA: But if I want to see my friends –

LEE: I'll say nothing. I'm begging you now – don't make
me beg.

MARINA: And I'll smoke when I want.

LEE: If you must.

MARINA: You won't call me lazy or – what is the word –
slut?

LEE: You'll come back?

MARINA: ... yes Lee.

> [*The stage darkens again. Their voices and their move-
> ments are swallowed up in the slow dark night.*]
>
> [*A spot fixes on* MARGUERITE. *She is a little more
> estranged from us. She is still talking and defending her son.
> She sees him as no other person close can see him. Yet the
> picture of him is so diffuse.*
>
> *She walks forward on the stage.*]

COMMISSION: ... Did he ever talk about re-enlisting
into the Marines after he returned?

MARGUERITE: Well, when Lee returned he was with me
three days, and then of course, he went over to visit
Robert's house. So actually we didn't talk.

COMMISSION: He said nothing about re-enlisting in the
Marines?

MARGUERITE: No. The three days he was home. That was the conversation – about him going on a ship. I saw his passport. And his passport was stamped 'import and export' on his passport.

COMMISSION: Did you know that he spoke Russian at that time, when he had the passport?

MARGUERITE: No sir I did not know . . . Now one thing I have forgotten. While at the State Department, the State Department told me that Lee had gone to Finland before Russia. And I did not know that. Now, Lee had applied at a college in Finland, evidently, because on the application it states such a fact. I did not know – because the paper just said he arrived in Russia – [*She waves a large white sheet of paper at the audience.*] . . . This is Lee's original application, that you cannot possibly have had. This is the only application there is. So this is something new for you gentlemen. I am not going to go through it all, because you have a copy. But I am going to show you the thinking of this young man. Special interests: religious, vocational, literary, sports and hobbies. Philosophy, psychology, ideology, football, baseball, tennis, stamp collecting. Lee had a stamp collecting book. Nature of private reading: Jack London, Darwin, Norman Vincent Peale, scientific books, philosophy and so on.

[*On the other side of the stage a spot picks up* MARINA's *face. She is further away from the front than her mother-in-law. She repeats a phrase she has already said.*]

MARINA: . . . It seemed peculiar to me and didn't want to believe it but he did not love his mother, she was not quite a normal woman. Now, I know this for sure.

[*The spot fades.* MARGUERITE *is still talking. The light is still on her.*]

COMMISSION: You think that he decided to defect after this application?

MARGUERITE: I do not know Sir because I have not had this from the boy. I am speculating. But I have a lot of documents to sustain my speculation.

COMMISSION: Now, this, you cannot tell one way or another about whether he is an agent by this?

MARGUERITE: I cannot tell by anything he is an agent, if you want proof. I am becoming a little discouraged about this, because I keep telling you – I did not have proof, Sir. But I am giving you documents leading to it.

COMMISSION: All that I am trying to find out is what you have. You are giving us that. I am also trying to find out whatever proof you have about these various things that we can rely on.

MARGUERITE: Well I am going to state once and for all, because it upsets me very much emotionally. And I have stated before, I do not have proof, Sir. I do not have proof of an agent. I do not have proof my son is innocent. I do not have proof.

COMMISSION: You don't have any proof of a conspiracy?

MARGUERITE: Of anything. It is just as I feel, like the Dallas Police do not have proof my son shot President Kennedy. If they have anything, it is circumstantial evidence. I have as much circumstantial evidence here that Lee was an agent as the Dallas police have that he shot President Kennedy.

ACT TWO

The stage is dark once more. Out of the black stillness on the stage MARINA *steps forward as the voice begins the questions again.*
The spot picks up her young rather pretty but certainly very Americanized features. She is very well dressed. In a sense one feels she is behaving too well. Her poise and compliance doesn't add up to her whole being.

COMMISSION: Could you tell us those things that you observed that caused you to think he had something in mind at that time, and I will ask you later, after you tell us, those that you discovered since or that you have obtained more light on since.

MARINA: At that time I did not think anything about it. I had no reasons to think that he had something in mind. I did not understand him at that time.

COMMISSION: Do you recall the first time that you observed the rifle?

MARINA: That was on Neely Street. I think that was in February 1963.

COMMISSION: How did you learn about it? Did you see it some place in the apartment?

MARINA: Yes, Lee had a small room where he spent a great deal of time, where he read – where he kept his things, and that is where the rifle was.

COMMISSION: Was it out in the room at that time, as distinguished from in a closet in the room?

MARINA: Yes it was open, out in the open. At first I think – I saw some package up on the top shelf, and I think that that was the rifle. But I didn't know. And apparently later he assembled it and had it in the room.

COMMISSION: When you saw the rifle assembled in the room, did it have the scope on it?

MARINA: No it did not have a scope on it.

COMMISSION: Did you have any discussion with your husband about the rifle when you first saw it?

MARINA: Of course I asked him . . .

[*The lights come up.* LEE *is on the floor on his knees. He has gun grease and polish and a barrel plunger before him. The gun is in pieces.*

LEE *is in a small room. A door is near to his arm.* MARINA *stands in the doorway looking down on him. He doesn't seem surprised. Then after she talks to him he becomes surprised and truculent. They talk in Russian.*]

MARINA: . . . Haven't I seen that before?

LEE: Depends . . . if you've been in and around here in my room – then you been smelling some haven't you? I mean by that – you been looking – and – Marina – in my room.

MARINA: I saw a parcel – last week –

LEE: But you looked inside my room. You only saw a parcel because you only could have seen a parcel if you had opened that door and peered in.

MARINA: So?

LEE: So . . . eh – you been peering in on my private life – my room that is.

MARINA: I'm sorry –

LEE: Too late.

MARINA: Lock it if you don't want me to see –

LEE: I don't.

MARINA: Buy a lock.

LEE: Can't afford it any.

MARINA: How much did that thing cost Lee?

LEE: If you had seen fit to understand how a man is –
you'd know you don't just bust in on his private
room – my room – and you'd know it is loyalty that
keeps it that way. Like I say. It's trust Marina ...

MARINA: How much Lee?

LEE: If you had trust Marina –

[MARINA *pulls his hair. She is very serious.*]

MARINA: What did I ask you?

LEE: And that's no good – didn't I say my hair was falling out – and you come and pull it! Now what quicker
way to have a man's hair all fall out than pull it
Marina – !

[MARINA *stands and waits and watches on him.*]

... It cost twenty-one dollars.

MARINA: Why?

LEE: Why? Because 'why' the rifle costs money? You
know it costs money!

MARINA: Why buy it? We're poor. I'd like – that
money, thank you. June would. Wouldn't she like
shoes? And you buy that!

LEE: I had one before –

MARINA: Russia's different –

LEE: There's hunting – handy for some hunting out of
town –

MARINA: That's not the point! You tell me Lee how
much things cost! A refrigerator costs that rifle, does
it?

LEE: If you like – a very old one that is –

MARINA: A suit for me and shoes and stockings – how
much?

LEE: I can't talk to you.

MARINA: And you buy this thing – and you polish it!

LEE: I said not to interfere in my private things – there's
squirrel and ducktail out there – that's all.

MARINA: Then I won't ask you any more.

LEE: Fine – well then you'll excuse me some.

MARINA: Is the rifle more interesting . . .

LEE: I thought I told you never to pull at my hair – that's what made me mad – now you're sore –

MARINA: No –

LEE: Putting it on me that you are –

MARINA: I – I can't understand you Lee – I try –

LEE: All I want is to be left see.

MARINA: And you don't love June and I –

LEE: I do. I told you I do.

MARINA: I'm trying to say – you are so different now.

LEE: Of course I am. When you do something that throws me yes I am. First it was my room – then it was pulling on my hair – and then, now, I mean – I remember other things which make life more difficult for me –

MARINA: Remember what?

LEE: Didn't I get out – by telling you you pulled at my hair – I recall when I bought that bottle of restorer –

MARINA: I don't understand you I don't understand you!

LEE: For my hair! Because – because it was falling out – I put it on the side table – and you fed June – and I was coming in and I saw you clear as day – try put that hair grease from that bottle – my restorer bottle – on June's rusk and you say what is it that has changed!

MARINA: But I didn't put that restorer on June's –

LEE: But I'm saying I thought you were then going on and about to put it!

[MARINA *is suddenly exhausted.*]

MARINA: Yes Lee.

LEE: And I'm saying I wouldn't have recalled the bad

things if you hadn't have brought them up by saying you been spying on me some.

MARINA: I'm tired now ... too much shouting ...

LEE: She is lazy and slow and she won't cook but she wants refrigerators and now she's tired and all!

MARINA: Can I ... do something for you. Can I do anything. I will. I apologize. I forget all about what I'm supposed to have done.... Can I? Anything now I'll do – ?

LEE: Now you're being cowardly.

MARINA: Name something –

LEE: All right. But no more games.

MARINA: No.

LEE: Ask me nothing ... I must breathe I must have a corner ... here is another thing ... [*He goes to a drawer. He pulls out an Imperial reflex camera. He hands it to her.*] Now I been putting all this together – like it is now – now you come out here – and I'll pose you. I'll pose for you and you take a picture – because I have another thing you must see – [*He opens another drawer. He pulls out a gun and a holster.*] ... I bought this too. Now this is a much better gun. The rifle is here – and it's ready and everything – and I put the gun on – and you come over here – [*He pulls her out to the front of the stage. He strikes a pose just like the Commission picture shows. And* MARINA *gingerly holds up the camera.*] Yes you are. It's loaded. Now come on. Wind it up to a new number – have you? Now – where's the sun Marina?

MARINA: Behind me.

LEE: That's the first right thing you haven't done wrong all day – !

[MARINA *takes two pictures. Click. Then rewind. Click.*]

I was thinking – you know what it was? There was

June – eating that hair restorer – as if you'd given it to her – and I had a dream about it – I had a dream – she ate it I always remember these things in retrospection – that's a long word – I hope it's right – I ain't never had it right in English – and I dreamt all her teeth – that is June's – came out all growing sprouting out with hairs and she looked like a walrus and she said –

[MARINA *begins to laugh.*]

What is funny Marina?

MARINA: I'm laughing that's all – [*She laughs out loud as if from great relief. As if some way of looking at* LEE *came clear to her.*]

LEE: I don't see why you should laugh – I have a serious psychological thing about hair and teeth – and hair and teeth are symbols of psychological importance –

[MARINA *is still laughing.*]

MARINA: Lee . . . I can't hold the camera.

LEE: And I know I'm worried . . . about decay and growth – and the fall of civilizations and . . . [*He just stares at her laughing.*]

MARINA: I can't help it . . . it's so impossible to understand you – oh . . . I'm really crying. Laughing and crying you see . . .

[LEE *still adopts his silly militaristic pose. He looks very wary and uncertain and slightly silly. As indeed* MARINA *sees him. She laughs and wipes her eyes.*]

LEE: If you would kindly tell me what's funny Marina – I'd laugh too maybe.

MARINA: You couldn't . . . oh you couldn't. That's what's so funny!

[*The stage falls away into blackness. No figures are distinguishable. Her laughter and* LEE's *strained surprise filter away. After a moment* MARINA *comes back up front. Her face is made clear by the spotlight. The voice asks her questions.*]

COMMISSION: Did you have anything to do with the prints of the photograph after the prints were made? That is, did you put them in a photograph album yourself?

MARINA: Lee gave me one photograph and asked me to keep it for June somewhere. Of course June doesn't need photographs like that.

COMMISSION: Do you recall how long after that the Walker matter occurred?

MARINA: Two perhaps three weeks later. I don't know. You know better when this happened.

COMMISSION: How did you first learn that your husband had shot at General Walker?

MARINA: That evening he went out, I thought that he had gone to his classes or perhaps that he just walked out or went out on his own business. It got to be about ten or ten thirty he wasn't home yet, and I began to be worried. Perhaps even later. Then I went into his room. Somehow – I was drawn to it – you know – I was pacing around. Then I saw a note there.

COMMISSION: Did you look for the gun at that time?

MARINA: No. I didn't understand anything. On the note it said – 'If I am arrested' and there are certain other questions such as for example, the key to the mailbox in such and such a place, and that he left me some money to last me for some time, and I couldn't understand at all what can he be arrested for. When he came back I asked him what had happened. He was very pale. I don't remember the exact time, but it was very late. And he told me not to ask him any questions. He only told me that he had shot at General Walker. Of course I didn't sleep all night. I thought that at any minute now the police will come. Of course I wanted to ask him a great deal. But in his state I decided I had best leave him alone – it would be purposeless to question him.

COMMISSION: Did he say any more than that about the shooting?

MARINA: Of course in the morning I told him that I was worried and that we can have a lot of trouble, and I asked him ...

[*The lights come up again.* LEE *is in bed. He appears asleep.* MARINA *walks across to the bed. She shakes the slumped shape of* LEE. *He stirs.*]

MARINA: ... Lee?

LEE: ... I'm asleep now.

MARINA: No ... Lee!

LEE: You won't find out Marina – because you wouldn't understand any – so don't ask me ...

MARINA: Where is the rifle?

LEE: You been snooping again –

MARINA: I looked in your room – and I looked under the bed –

LEE: Snooping some ...

[MARINA *turns him out of bed. She rolls him and his blankets like a white cotton sausage across the floor.*]

MARINA: We'll all be killed we'll be thrown out – and we won't ever come back! Now speak to me!

[LEE *slowly disentangles himself from the sheets.*]

LEE: I hid it ...

MARINA: Where?

LEE: Buried it ...

MARINA: Did you kill the man?

LEE: You didn't – wait! – there, Marina, you didn't ask me where I buried the rifle.

68

MARINA: Oh – well?

LEE: I put it under trees and earth in the highway – in a back lot – where no dogs would smell it. Dogs can find an object anywhere – but earth – just damp natural and ordinary earth beats the smell.

MARINA: Kill kill!

LEE: No – I don't know – I guess I did – I don't know.

MARINA: And that's all?

LEE: You wouldn't understand any if I was to sit down and explain it – so I'm not going to waste my time Marina.

MARINA: You had no right –

LEE: No – but I did it.

MARINA: Why?

LEE: I tell you – like this – do you hear of the American Fact Finding Committee?

MARINA: No.

LEE: Hear of Mr Stevenson coming to Dallas?

MARINA: No.

LEE: Hear of people not wanting him to come?

MARINA: No.

LEE: Hear of fascists and fascism?

MARINA: Yes – they're bad people –

LEE: One mark! Out of a hundred! Hear of anti-semites? And of anti-communists?

MARINA: Yes and – no.

LEE: Then I can't tell you why.

MARINA: Why what?

LEE: I've just told you that's why – why what! – told you that's why what and you won't understand any because you just told me just now didn't you – you say no and no.

MARINA: You can't kill a man – because he thinks differently to you.

LEE: Did I kill him?

MARINA: I don't know.

LEE: But you just said – [*He pulls pants over his pajamas pants. Dresses hurriedly.*]

MARINA: I'm asking you Lee.

LEE: That's the point – I better go get a paper – did you hear the news on the radio?

MARINA: I'm too scared.

LEE: I'm going on out – get the papers. I'll be back.

MARINA: But Lee ...

[LEE *stubs his feet into his shoes and leaves.*]

LEE: But Lee!

MARINA: Suppose he's dead!

LEE: Hell – I can't be that good a shot. [*He runs out.*]

[*The darkness descends on the stage.* MARINA *picks up a piece of white bed linen. She just stands holding it staring at it. After some moments,* MARINA *comes back up front. She is still answering questions. The single spotlight picks her up. It is obviously hard work and she is beginning to tire of questions and answer.*]

COMMISSION: After he shot at Walker, did you notice his taking the rifle out any more to practise?

MARINA: No.

COMMISSION: Do you recall when he went to New Orleans?

MARINA: I think it was in May. Lee went there himself, by himself. At that time, I became acquainted with Mrs Paine, and I stayed with her while he was looking for work. In about one week Lee telephoned me that he had found a job and that I should come down.

COMMISSION: Did you then leave at once for New Orleans?

MARINA: Yes.

COMMISSION: At New Orleans, who did your husband work for?

MARINA: He worked for the Louisiana Coffee Company. But I don't know in what capacity. I don't think that this was very good job, or perhaps more correctly, he did not – I know that he didn't like this job.

COMMISSION: How long did he work for this coffee company?

MARINA: I think it was from May until August, to the end of August.

COMMISSION: And then he was unemployed for a time?

MARINA: Yes.

[*The stage lightens.* LEE *is sitting very stiffly on a porch verandah in their flat. He holds his rifle between his knees. He just sits like a stone.* MARINA *is walking around, doing small things. She suddenly notices him there. She stands and stares strangely. He doesn't look at her. He doesn't move.*]

MARINA: Lee?

[*It is an early warm evening. The window to the porch is open. Warm summer sounds come in.*]

Lee – is that meant to be some kind of a joke?

LEE: No.

MARINA: Well why don't you come in?

LEE: I'm thinking.

MARINA: Oh.

LEE: You know – think like thought.

MARINA: I know Lee. Perhaps you'd tell me some of them?

LEE: I – no.

MARINA: Please Lee.

LEE: I was thinking about my books. But you never read them.

MARINA: I don't think that I was ever allowed to.

LEE: My books are about Washington, and Disraeli, and Kerensky – and then there's de Gaulle and Truman – now you don't read those books.

MARINA: What do they say Lee?

LEE: They show how a guy can become President – can show his country the way –

MARINA: Oh yes.

LEE: I'm going to find a way. I could become – it all takes time – but there is no reason why I shouldn't be President of the United States in twenty years.

MARINA: How?

LEE: I'm saying there ain't no reason – none at all –

MARINA: I don't understand –

LEE: There is no reason why I shouldn't –

MARINA: What reason Lee?

LEE: I'm saying there's no reason at all – that's all.

MARINA: But you're no different from anyone –

LEE: I know that.

MARINA: Well then –

LEE: I know that and sure. It's that – I *feel* different – and if there ain't no reason why such things happen and people become important and famous – there ain't no reason why it won't be me.

MARINA: You just sit there – and pretend ... is that what you do?

LEE: You don't think things possible – because you don't think on them hard see – but I do – now I was *thinking* if I were to hijack a plane to Cuba – a good a real good plane and I'd stick the pilot with a pistol – he'd sure go there fast enough – then they'd pay attention to me ... say that I'm a friend. I've got contacts now – my political allies write me from the North. But you wouldn't know about that ...

MARINA: Why are you getting these letters from New York?

LEE: I am Chapter – for an organization.

MARINA: Oh – which?

LEE: Fair Play for Cuba.

MARINA: When are you going to work again?

LEE: When the unemployment money runs out. Meanwhile, I've got a job, I have an office, and I have printed headed notepaper which says Fair Play for Cuba – and you wouldn't understand.

MARINA: No – I wouldn't.

LEE: That's what I'm saying. And I'm saying something else – I want to take a trip – I have to go to Mexico City – because after all this work I've done for Cuba – when I go there – I'll get a visa – for Cuba – and I'll help them –

MARINA: Without me –

LEE: I'll come back before the cash runs down. [*It is obvious* LEE *won't communicate with her. He is talking more to himself. Nothing she says cuts much ice in his mind.*]

MARINA: I can't stay here. I'll take June back to Dallas.

LEE: Yeah.

MARINA: Ruth Paine will have us. [*She goes across to him. She takes the rifle from his still hands. She puts it on the table. All this is done very gently. The lack of contact fills the air between them.*] You don't need this – if you go to Mexico ...

[LEE *bows his head. He seems deeply upset.*]

LEE: No.

[MARINA *comes back to him. She touches his head. He won't move.*]

MARINA: Don't cry ... Lee ... things will be better things will be constant one day ... I'm not nagging you. [*Very gently she unstraps the pistol belt and holster from his waist. He is so hurt inside he cannot move. She puts it on the floor.*]

LEE: ... You wouldn't understand ...

MARINA: I try ... [*She unlaces and pulls off of him his heavy boots. They seem ridiculous and military and it is hot anyway.*]

LEE: The jobs – why do I lose them? ... It would be much easier Marina in Russia – we wouldn't have to worry about tomorrow all the time – they look after you – you get work – all the time – and the State cares – the State wants you well and able – and here – it's run and jump – I been doing all of that – and – we get – a room and a television set – each time it's a start everything starts but it never finishes – that's what I'm saying. [*He is terribly sad and ill about it. It's difficult to see if he cries or not, he hides his face.* MARINA *kneels in front of him by the open window looking out on the New Orleans street.*] When I told you in Minsk America was beautiful when I said it was wide open and exciting – I didn't tell you the truth. Nobody here takes care of you – you die here and it's only one less – you die in Russia and the State has lost an ally a friend ...

MARINA: Come to bed ...

LEE: Why?

MARINA: Come to bed and make love to me –

LEE: No Marina – you will never understand – I don't want to do that any more –

MARINA: Just sleep then –

LEE: Sleep is funny ... I don't dream no more – I can't remember – but I know I'm sure – it's a black space now.

[*The darkness again. Quite quickly* MARINA *comes up front. The questions continue. She answers in a detached fashion. After all she has already been over this ground with the F.B.I. It is a repeat performance she doesn't enjoy.*]

COMMISSION: Did your husband stay with you at the Paines' after that first night when he returned from Mexico?

MARINA: Yes he stayed overnight there. And in the morning we took him to Dallas.

COMMISSION: And by 'we' who do you mean?

MARINA: Ruth Paine, I and her children.

COMMISSION: Do you know what he did in Dallas then?

MARINA: He intended to rent an apartment in the area of Oak Cliff, and to look for work.

COMMISSION: Do you know whether he did that?

MARINA: Yes I know that he always tried to get some work. He was not lazy.

COMMISSION: Did he rent the apartment?

MARINA: On the same day he rented a room, not an apartment, and he telephoned me and told me about it.

COMMISSION: Did you discuss the plans for this room before you took him to Dallas?

MARINA: No, I asked him where he would live and he said it would be best if he rented a room, it would not be as expensive as an apartment.

COMMISSION: Did he say anything about whether you should be living with him, or he would be living there alone?

MARINA: No, I did not really want to be with Lee at that time, because I was expecting, and it would have been better to be with a woman who spoke Russian and English.

COMMISSION: Do you know where your husband looked for work in Dallas at that time?

MARINA: No. He tried to get any kind of work. He answered ads, newspaper ads.

COMMISSION: Did he have trouble finding work again?

MARINA: Yes.

COMMISSION: Did you discuss with him possible places of employment after his return from Mexico?

MARINA: No that was his business. I couldn't help him in that. But to some extent I did help him find a job, because I was visiting Mrs Paine's neighbours, there was a woman there who told me where he might find some work.

COMMISSION: And who was it that you got the information from?

MARINA: It was the neighbour whose brother was employed by the school book depository. He said it seemed to him there was a vacancy there.

COMMISSION: What was his name?

MARINA: I don't know.

COMMISSION: Mrs Oswald I do not ask these questions to pry into your personal affairs, but it gives us some insight into what he did and why he might have done the things he did . . . I hope you understand that.

MARINA: I understand.

COMMISSION: Could you tell us a little about when he did beat you because we have reports that at times neighbours saw signs of his having beat you, so that we might know the occasions and why he did such things.

MARINA: The neighbours simply saw that because I have a very sensitive skin, and even a very light blow would show marks. Sometimes it was my own fault. Sometimes it was really necessary to just leave him alone. But I wanted more attention. He was jealous. He had no reason to be. But he was jealous of even some of my old friends, old in the sense of age.

COMMISSION: When he became jealous did he discuss that with you?

MARINA: Yes of course.

COMMISSION: What did he say?

[*The stage lights up.* MARINA *is washing dishes. There is a knock on the door. Then a frantic knocking. She opens the door. It is* LEE. *If possible* MARINA *must appear pregnant at this time.*]

LEE: I want to talk ...

MARINA: You can phone me.

LEE: I went to my post box this evening –

MARINA: Lee if you're going to start a quarrel – remember – Ruth is in this house and she is coming back and –

LEE: I want some truth!

MARINA: Yes?

LEE: Sit ... sit ... [*He shoves her into a chair at a table. He takes the other chair and faces her across the table. He fetches an airmail letter and envelope out of the pocket in his jacket.*]

MARINA: I can't be made excited – I am about to have the baby –

LEE: You did not have my permission to use that box number of mine in the Dallas Post Office! Right – one! Two – this letter came back to the post box – today – two! And three – I read it ...

MARINA: It – it was a joke –

LEE: I'll read it –

MARINA: It was – so help me – I'm telling you!

LEE: Dear Friend from out of the Russian past – when you asked me to marry you before I left Minsk – I made a big mistake – I remember how much you loved me – you said so –

MARINA: He was not my lover –

LEE: I am so happy to remember what it was like in the snow in the cold when we had nothing but fur boots and old woollen garments under our raincoats – here I am so miserable nothing ever seems to go right –

people are not my friends – I move house too often –

MARINA: I was telling the truth –

LEE: I was a fool not to have married you – but now I cannot retrace my footsteps –

MARINA: Yes all right! I wrote it! . . . Damn you! Do you blame me – isn't it the truth – there is so little love between us?

LEE: Who was he – I mean is he?

MARINA: He loved me – once.

LEE: Behind my back – and let me tell you how I came by it you made one little mistake – you forgot the Texas postage duty has raised itself up one cent – last week! That's why they returned the letter to the box. My box!

MARINA: I have nothing to say. Except – he was a man and he loved me.

LEE: Why do you write to him?

MARINA: You tell me to leave you alone you tell me to go back to Russia that I'll be happier there – that there is nothing here in this huge vast country but small pay and your little jobs – now I begin to believe you!

LEE: But it's immoral to do that to me – write to him here – I'm your husband.

MARINA: Does it really still look like it to you Lee?

LEE: I try – I get work – I try.

MARINA: I have written letters before –

LEE: To him!

MARINA: To the embassy in Washington – I take your advice I see it is hopeless – something drives you you fight everything – you hate at any given moment – there is no place for me in your life –

LEE: Tell me this – did you mean it sincere? All that letter?

[MARINA *pauses. She is afraid.*]

78

MARINA: ... Yes.

[LEE *hits her across her head and hair. She sways.*]

LEE: Did you mean it for true?

MARINA: Yes ...

[LEE *slaps her face very hard. The sound rings.*]

MARINA: ... I deserve it ... all right ... I do.

LEE: There's more Marina ... [*He stands up.*]

[MARINA *jumps clear and backs away.*]

MARINA: I have a baby now – you won't hit me again –

LEE: I've got to do something to you –

MARINA: Do anything – love me – do anything – but
don't hit Marina – Alek!

[LEE *aims to hit her. She ducks away. She picks up a small
portable radio. She hits him with it on the skull.* LEE *falls
and catches his breath.*]

LEE: ... Alek?

MARINA: I'm sorry ...

LEE: Alek you called me ...

MARINA: I always thought you were Alek when we first
met – that was why.

LEE: That was years ago ...

MARINA: Yes ... I forget it all now ...

LEE: You see ... don't you ... how jealous I am ... [*He
seems like a child now. The energy has gone. He almost wants
an adult's affection. He is self-righteous and suddenly rather
soft and sullen.*]

MARINA: Of what Lee?

LEE: Our relationship.

MARINA: I wouldn't let you hit me – I think more of the
baby than of you – what relationship is there now?

LEE: None – it seems all to have gone away ... where did
it go Marina – remember – and will you please tell me?

[*Then hold that: The stage darkens: Pause: Then*
MARINA *comes forward: Spotlight.*]

COMMISSION: Did your husband continue to call you daily from Dallas after he got his job?

MARINA: Yes.

COMMISSION: Did he tell you what he was doing?

MARINA: Usually he would call me during the lunch-break and the second time after he was finished work, and he told me that he was reading, that he was watching television, and sometimes I told him that he should not stay in his room too much, that he should go for a walk in the park.

COMMISSION: Have you ever heard that he used the fictitious name Hidell?

MARINA: Yes.

COMMISSION: Did you think he was using that assumed name in connexion with this Fair Play for Cuba activity or something else?

MARINA: The name Hidell (Fidel) which you pronounce Hidell, was in connexion with his activity with the non-existing organization.

COMMISSION: Now during the week of the assassination did your husband call you at all by telephone?

MARINA: He telephoned me on Monday, after I had called him on Sunday, and he was not there. Or rather, he was there but he wasn't called to the phone because he was known by another name. On Monday he called several times, but after I hung up on him and didn't want to talk to him he did not call again. He then arrived on Thursday.

COMMISSION: Did you learn he was using the assumed name of Lee as his last name?

MARINA: I know it now, but I did not ever know it before.

COMMISSION: Thursday was the 21st do you recall that?

MARINA: Yes.

COMMISSION: And the assassination was on the 22nd.

MARINA: This is very hard to forget.

COMMISSION: Did your husband give any reason for coming home on Thursday?

MARINA: He said that he was lonely because he hadn't come the preceding week-end, and he wanted to make his peace with me.

[*The stage lights up again.* MARINA *walks to a line. She stretches the line right across the stage and carefully places dozens of wet nappies on the line.* LEE *enters.*]

LEE: ... Hi ... Marina ...

MARINA: Don't tread on the diapers ...

LEE: I wasn't ...

MARINA: You might.

LEE: ... I said Hi ... Marina ...

MARINA: No 'Hi' Lee.

LEE: Means what?

MARINA: What I say.

LEE: Won't talk to me?

MARINA: No.

LEE: Well ... I took the bus for an hour to come over here.

MARINA: Sure you did.

LEE: So that's an effort.

MARINA: I'm using Ruth's line in her kitchen to hang up diapers – that's one too.

LEE: Sure.

MARINA: ... Sure.

LEE: But you won't talk –

MARINA: You know why I hung up – earlier –

LEE: No not really.

MARINA: Lee's not your real name –

LEE: No.

MARINA: Why tell lies about it?

LEE: I'm not hiding like – there's something immoral –

MARINA: Sometimes I wish there were! I'd understand you better.

LEE: I have to keep myself to myself –

MARINA: Surely. You do that.

LEE: I can't explain –

MARINA: Why didn't you come home over here – last week-end – ?

LEE: I thought you didn't want to see me.

MARINA: Do I now?

LEE: Marina ... what if I were to get an apartment more in town – for us all –

MARINA: It's cheaper here. I don't spend your money.

LEE: What if – well the job's steady – I'll make peace with you Marina –

MARINA: Mind the laundry –

LEE: There'll be no more hitting you –

MARINA: There is no more – anyway.

LEE: I don't – I don't see any need why you should stay with Ruth – she ain't my friend –

MARINA: She's mine – she's good.

LEE: Look – haven't I played with the kids before? Course I have. Can I work regular – if they'll only let me hold on – sure I work. I want Rachel with me – and I want June – and you –

MARINA: You said it Lee – the hitting me, the rows, that gun thing and the Cuba – what happened with the visa? What has happened to me – do I go back – do I still apply to go home – and this name game – if you can't explain it who can? I'm tired Lee ... be ordinary be normal be human – and something might happen – but everything falls apart and you can't see it!

[LEE *tries to move towards her. She ducks under the line. He pushes through it and pulls it down. The whole line. After she so carefully put it up. He treads clumsily on the wet nappies.*]

LEE: Oh Marina – I'm in a mess – I can't step over them – [*They drape around him like a rash of wet white naval pennants.*]

MARINA: You see ... how can I live? You're in a mess – yes – but see how I live – if you want a hope – one brass hope in hell of getting me back – I want a machine –

LEE: A machine?

MARINA: I want one of those large white washing machines – with a heater – with a spinner and a washing tub – and the electric wire and socket to make it work in – and then perhaps you won't tread all over my work! [*She furiously unravels the nappies from him. She strips them away from him. She gathers up the line.*] That's it.

LEE: Then you'll have me?

MARINA: Maybe – the machine comes first.

LEE: That hurts – Marina.

MARINA: Good.

LEE: I try ...

MARINA: Do it harder.

LEE: Is that all?

MARINA: There is no food to offer you.

LEE: I didn't mean that –

MARINA: I'm taking a bath – then I'm going to bed ...

LEE: Oh I see.

MARINA: Goodnight Lee ...

LEE: I'll be gone in the morning ...

MARINA: Yes I know.

LEE: Gone early.

MARINA: I won't be awake.

LEE: ... No.

[*They stand and stare at each other. The light closes around them. The stage is dark now. Then after some seconds* MARINA *walks up front. The questions start.*]

COMMISSION: What did you do the rest of the morning after you got up on November 22nd?

MARINA: When I got up the television set was on, and I knew that Kennedy was coming. Ruth had gone to the doctor with her children and she left the television set on for me. And I watched television all morning, even without having dressed. June was running around in her pajamas watching television with me.

COMMISSION: Before the assassination did you ever see your husband examining the route of the parade as it was published in the paper?

MARINA: No.

COMMISSION: Did you ever see him looking at a map of Dallas like he did in connexion with the Walker shooting?

MARINA: No.

COMMISSION: How did you learn of the shooting of President Kennedy?

MARINA: I was watching television, and Ruth by that time was already with me, and she said someone had shot at the President.

COMMISSION: What did you say?

MARINA: It was hard for me to say anything. We both turned pale. I went to my room and cried.

COMMISSION: Did you think immediately that your husband might have been involved?

MARINA: No.

COMMISSION: Did Mrs Paine say anything about the possibility of your husband being involved?

MARINA: No, but she only said that 'by the way, they fired from the building in which Lee is working'. . . .

My heart dropped. I then went to the garage to see whether the rifle was there, and I saw that the blanket was still there, and I said 'thank God'. I thought 'can there really be such a stupid man in the world that could do something like that?' But I was already rather upset at that time – I don't know why. Perhaps my intuition. I didn't know what I was doing.

COMMISSION: Did you look in the blanket to see if the rifle was there?

MARINA: I didn't unroll the blanket. It was in its usual position and it appeared to have something inside.

COMMISSION: When did you learn that the rifle was not in the blanket?

MARINA: When the police arrived and asked whether my husband had a rifle, and I said 'yes'.

COMMISSION: When the police came did Mrs Paine act as an interpreter for you?

MARINA: Yes.

COMMISSION: Did the police spend considerable time there?

MARINA: Yes.

COMMISSION: Did they want you to go with them?

MARINA: Yes.

COMMISSION: Did you leave the house with them right after they came?

MARINA: About an hour I think.

COMMISSION: And what were they doing during that hour?

MARINA: They searched the entire house.

COMMISSION: Did you see or speak to your husband on November 22nd following his arrest?

MARINA: On the 22nd I did not see him. On the 23rd I met with him.

COMMISSION: Did you request the right to see your husband on the 22nd after his arrest?

MARINA: Yes.

COMMISSION: And what answer were you given at that time?

MARINA: I was not permitted to.

COMMISSION: Where did you spend the evening on the night of the assassination?

MARINA: On the day of the assassination, on the 22nd, after returning from questioning by the police, I spent the night with Mrs Paine, together with Lee's mother. [*She stands still. She is now very edgy and upset. The blow of* LEE *and his arrest shows in her. She breaks out from beneath this slow calm innocent and hesitant manner. Her emotions begin to bleed a little.*]

[*Opposite her, on the other side of the stage, there is* MARGUERITE. *She comes forward. The spot picks out her broad wrinkled troubled face. Much of the earlier confidence has left her too. The questions are directed at* MARGUERITE.]

MARGUERITE: ... So then ... the next thing we should start then ... would be the Dallas ... the assassination.

COMMISSION: Whatever you know.

MARGUERITE: Well, I was on a case in a rest home, and I had a three to eleven shift. I was dressed. Ready to go to work. I was watching – I'm a little ahead of my story, I watched the television in the morning before I was dressed. And Richard Nixon was in Dallas, and he made a television appearance approximately two hours before President Kennedy was to arrive in Dallas. And, as a layman, I remember saying – 'well, the audacity of him, to make this statement against President Kennedy just an hour or two before his arrival in Dallas'. And then I had my lunch, and I dressed, with my nurses' uniform on, to go to work, for the three to eleven shift. And I have to leave home at 2.30. So I had a little time to watch the Presidential procession. And while sitting on the sofa the news came that the President was shot. And there was a witness on television, a man and a little girl on television. However I could not continue to watch it. I had to report to work. So I went in the car, and approximately seven blocks away I turned the radio on in the car. I heard that Lee Harvey Oswald was picked up as a suspect. I immediately turned the car around and came back home, got on the telephone, called Acme Brick in Fort Worth, and asked where Robert was, because he had been travelling, and I must get in touch with Robert immediately, because his brother was picked up as a suspect in the assassination. So they had Robert call me. Robert didn't know that Lee was picked up.

COMMISSION: Was this the day of the assassination?

MARGUERITE: Yes sir. The day of the assassination they picked Lee up.

COMMISSION: And three to eleven – that is in the afternoon?

MARGUERITE: This was 2.30 because I was on my way to work, and I had to be at work at 3 o'clock.

COMMISSION: Three in the afternoon is when you had to be at work?

MARGUERITE: Yes sir. And it was 2.30 I heard the news and went back home. I had Acme Brick call Robert to give him the news, and Robert called me, and he had not heard his brother was picked up. Now Robert is in Denton. So I called the *Star Telegram* and asked that – if they could possibly have someone escort me to

Dallas, because I realized I could not drive to Dallas. And they did. They sent two men to escort me to Dallas. The name of one is Bob Shieffer, the other name I will have for you gentlemen.

COMMISSION: Who are those? Are those reporters?

MARGUERITE: *Star Telegram* reporters, sent by the *Star Telegram* Editor to escort me to Dallas. Now upon arriving in Dallas, I did not ask – I did not want to talk to the police. I asked specifically to talk to F.B.I. agents. My wish was granted. I was sent into a room. I have to backtrack my story. The policemen do not know I'm here – 'I want to talk to F.B.I. agents!'

COMMISSION: This is approximately three thirty.

MARGUERITE: So I am escorted into an office, and two Brown F.B.I. agents, they are brothers, I understand, and there was another man that I do not know the name.

COMMISSION: By that you mean that their names were Brown?

MARGUERITE: Their names were Brown. And I have the correct names, also. But we were in this room, and I told them who I was. And I said 'I want to talk with you gentlemen because I feel like my son is an agent of the government. And for the security of my country, I don't want this to get out'.... But, first I said to them, 'I want to talk to F.B.I. agents from Washington' ... 'Mrs Oswald, we are from Washington, we work with Washington'. I said, 'I understand you work with Washington. But I want officials from Washington', – and I believed they would be in town because of protecting the President. I said – 'I do not want local F.B.I. men. What I have to say I want to say to Washington men'. Of course, they wanted the news. They said 'well, we work through Washington'.

I said – 'I know you do. But I would like Washington men.' So I had no choice.

COMMISSION: Did you tell them why you thought he was an agent?

MARGUERITE: Yes sir, I am coming to this. . . . So I said 'I have information that' – I told him who I was. I said – 'for the security of my country, I want this kept perfectly quiet until you investigate. I happen to know that the State Department furnished the money for my son to return back to the United States, and I don't know if that would be made public what that would involve, and so please will you investigate this and keep this quiet.' . . . Of course that was news to them . . . They left me sitting in the office . . . [*She seems to blurt all this out. As if she is hurried, as if something goads her along, words she feels she has to gobble out.*]

[*The stage becomes bright again. It is* RUTH PAINE'S *home.* MARINA *is there sitting very sadly. The television set flickers dully.* MARGUERITE *hasn't seen* MARINA *for a year.* MARINA *speaks her pidgin English to* MARGUERITE. MARINA *has picked up English fairly well. She does seem to understand what people mean. Perhaps she doesn't understand when she doesn't want to know a point.*]

MARGUERITE: . . . Marina?

MARINA: Yes – Mamma.

MARGUERITE: I came as quick as I could.

MARINA: Oh yes.

MARGUERITE: Have you been crying?

MARINA: All day . . .

MARGUERITE: I have too.

MARINA: They all came here.

MARGUERITE: Who 'they' honey?

MARINA: The officers.

MARGUERITE: The police?

MARINA: They come ... bang bang – all noise.

MARGUERITE: Now it's quiet.

MARINA: Yes Mamma.

MARGUERITE: Do you need any help?

MARINA: No.

MARGUERITE: Some food – cook a meal?

MARINA: No thank you.

MARGUERITE: He didn't do it – my Lee never done.

MARINA: Mamma – he had gun.

MARGUERITE: Everybody has a gun in Dallas –

MARINA: And he had mind – gone!

MARGUERITE: Don't you let them talk you in on anything –

[MARINA *gets up. She crosses to a shelf. On the shelf is a thick book. She takes a photograph out from the book. She hands it to* MARGUERITE.]

MARINA: Mamma – I show you.

MARGUERITE: Did you take that?

MARINA: Me.

MARGUERITE: Holding this rifle and all – and the pistol –

MARINA: Read it Mamma.

MARGUERITE: It says – to my daughter June.

MARINA: Yes.

MARGUERITE: Have you shown this anyone?

MARINA: No. You take it Mamma –

MARGUERITE: No.

MARINA: You have it –

MARGUERITE: No Marina ... put it back in the book. Please.

[MARINA *does so. Silently.*]

MARINA: Mamma – you stay here with me? Yes.

MARGUERITE: Yes – thank you.

MARINA: Ruth won't mind.

MARGUERITE: Marina – have you seen him?

MARINA: No.

MARGUERITE: Has he got a lawyer – he's a member of Civil Liberties.

MARINA: I don't know.

MARGUERITE: Do you want to see him honey?

[MARINA *doesn't answer. As if she hasn't heard the question. She looks back at her mother-in-law. She doesn't say a word. The stage darkens.* MARINA *stands forefront. The questions begin again.*]

COMMISSION: But from what you have learned since that time you arrived at this conclusion, did you, that your husband had killed the President?

MARINA: Yes, unfortunately, yes.

COMMISSION: And you related those facts that you learned to what you already knew about your life with him and what you knew he had done and appeared to be doing in order to come to that conclusion?

MARINA: Yes.

COMMISSION: When you saw your husband on November 23rd, at the police station, did you ask him if he had killed the President?

[MARINA *steps back into the stage. We can see* LEE *standing behind a glass wall. He looks lost and rather unkempt. Very haggard.* MARGUERITE *stands near to* MARINA. MARINA *approaches* LEE *first. She picks up the communicating telephone.*]

MARINA: ... Hallo Lee ...

LEE: Hallo.

MARINA: I tried to see you yesterday ...

LEE: Yes I know. I guessed.

MARINA: Hallo Lee – June is well ...

LEE: Don't worry don't worry ... don't cry.

MARINA: I love you. ...

LEE: Good. Fine.

MARINA: There is love?

LEE: From me? Sure ... yes.

MARINA: I don't believe ... that you did that – and everything –

LEE: I know what you're trying to say –

MARINA: Everything – everything will turn out – well.

LEE: Yes.

MARINA: And I love –

LEE: I do. I do.

MARINA: I hear you ...

LEE: Don't worry about a thing – as you say – it will all turn out – hear me?

[MARINA *puts the phonepiece down, and walks away from the glass wall. She stands apart and away.* MARGUERITE *walks up to the glass wall.*]

MARGUERITE: ... Honey you are so bruised up. Your face. What are they doing?

LEE: Mother don't worry now. I got that in a scuffle.

MARGUERITE: Is there anything I can do to help you?

LEE: No, Mother. Everything is fine. I know my rights. And I will have an attorney. I have already requested to get in touch with Attorney Abt, – I think is the name. Don't worry about a thing.

MARGUERITE: I won't ask you a thing Lee ... I am with you that's all.

LEE: I didn't do it Mother – I didn't do it. Now go home – tell Marina to buy June new shoes – go home – go now.

[*They all three leave the stage. After a pause* MARINA *walks back in on her own. The lights go down. A light centres on* MARINA.]

COMMISSION: Do you know whether he was ever acting as an undercover agent for the F.B.I.?

MARINA: No.

COMMISSION: Do you believe that he was at any time?

MARINA: No.

COMMISSION: Do you know whether or not he was acting as an agent for the C.I.A. at any time?

MARINA: No.

COMMISSION: Do you believe that he was?

MARINA: No.

COMMISSION: Did you know Jack Ruby, the man that killed your husband?

MARINA: No.

COMMISSION: Before the murder of your husband by Jack Ruby, had you ever known him?

MARINA: No, never.

COMMISSION: Do you know whether your husband knew Jack Ruby before the killing?

MARINA: He was not acquainted with him. Lee did not frequent nightclubs, as the papers said.

COMMISSION: How do you know that?

MARINA: He was always with me. He doesn't like other women. He didn't drink. Why should he then go?

COMMISSION: Do you know any reason why Jack Ruby killed your husband?

MARINA: About that, Jack Ruby should be questioned.

COMMISSION: I have to ask you Mrs Oswald.

MARINA: He didn't tell me.

[*From the other side of the stage* MARGUERITE *comes forward. The light fades on* MARINA. MARGUERITE *is talking. She is trying to make something clear, something which to her is very important. She seems excited as if she has discovered the truth.*]

MARGUERITE: ... now just a minute gentlemen, because this I know is very important to me and to you, too. We had been in the jail. This was an evening.

Well this then would be approximately five thirty or six in the evening.

COMMISSION: What day?

MARGUERITE: On Saturday November 23.

COMMISSION: That was at the Executive Inn?

MARGUERITE: At the Executive Inn. Now Mr Hart Odum, the F.B.I. agent, knocked on the door at the Executive Inn. I had my robe and slippers on, and I pushed the curtain aside when he knocked. He said 'this is Mr Odum'. I opened the door just a little, because I had the robe off and I didn't want anybody to come in. He said 'Mrs Oswald we would like to see Marina'. I said 'Mr Odum I am not calling my daughter. As a matter of fact she is taking a bath'. She wasn't. He said 'Mrs Oswald I would like to ask you a question'. The door is ajar. I wear bifocals which enlarges things. And in his hand – in the cup of his hand, like this is a picture. He said 'have you ever seen this man before?'

[*The lights are on the whole stage area.* MARGUERITE *walks to the door. She is wearing a nightrobe. She speaks to the far side of the door. Opposite her* MARINA *is unrolling a pair of stockings from her legs. She has no apparent interest in the conversation at the door.*]

MARGUERITE: ... Mr Odum ... I stated yesterday you are not going to see Marina.

[*There is a muffled sound of a male voice behind the door.*] You see – we are awful tired. Now you see.

[*Again the sound of a man's inquiring voice.*] As a matter of fact she is taking a bath. [*She seems to take a clear black and white photograph from behind the door. She looks at it carefully. The muffled male voice continues. She hands the photograph back behind the door.*] ... No Sir ... believe me. I have never seen this picture in my life.

[*She closes the door. She leans against it. She looks across at* MARINA. MARINA *totally unconcerned inspects the ladders in her stockings. The light fades again.*]

    [MARGUERITE *walks up front. She talks again to the* COMMISSION.]

COMMISSION: Could we get what picture this is? Is that the picture held in the hand?

MARGUERITE: Yes Sir – the picture that is held in the hand, that the F.B.I. agent Mr Hart Odum showed me.

COMMISSION: I understand you didn't recognize who the picture was at all.

MARGUERITE: No. I told Mr Hart Odum I had never seen the man before – 'believe me sir' – and he left. So the picture was shown – was tried – had tried to be shown to my daughter-in-law but they were not successful. Now I am under the impression since I know it was Mr Jack Ruby's picture I saw – at the time I didn't.

COMMISSION: How do you know that?

MARGUERITE: I have seen his picture in the paper. Now I know it is Mr Jack Ruby.

COMMISSION: What was the date now?

MARGUERITE: This Saturday November 23rd. This is approximately 6.30 in the evening that the F.B.I. agent came. And the telephone call was later. Now I have no way of knowing whether Lee had permission to use the phone, remember Lee is in jail.

COMMISSION: About what time do you think that telephone call was?

MARGUERITE: I would say it was about 7.30, 8 o'clock in the night.

COMMISSION: That was still on Saturday night?

MARGUERITE: Yes sir. Still on Saturday night at the

Executive Inn. And that was after the picture was shown to me – she received this telephone call, and became very silent. And the next day my son was shot.

COMMISSION: Do I understand correctly that Marina did not see the picture at any time?

MARGUERITE: That is correct sir. But they tried awfully hard for Marina to see the picture.

COMMISSION: And when they could not show it to her –

MARGUERITE: – they showed it to me – yes sir.

COMMISSION: Have you ever seen that picture since?

MARGUERITE: – Lee was shot on a Sunday – neither Marina nor I knew how he was shot. They kept it from us. You have to visualize this. We were at the Six Flags Motel with approximately eighteen to twenty F.B.I. agents, secret service men running in and out a woman with a Russian girl and two sick babies, and the girl and I do not know what is going on.

COMMISSION: Now, about what time on that Sunday did you learn of your son's death?

MARGUERITE: Well now, here is your time element. I said Robert and Mr Gregory and the Secret Service were there approximately from 11.30. And I knew nothing about the shooting. And then we had to go to Irving and everything. Then they told us Lee was shot. So now we are bringing up to the time – it all fits in – which was 1 o'clock or 1.30. And they were all watching the sequence on television ...

[*The stage lightens.* MARGUERITE *goes across to a TV set which is flickering. It stays on the exit in the Dallas Police Carport and basement where Lee Oswald was to be taken out to a waiting car.* MARGUERITE *sits down on what looks like a very plain piece of hotel-type Motel kind of seating arrangement. The TV set flickers. An American*

96

voice says out loud 'And here he is. Here is Lee Harvey Oswald. Lee Harvey Oswald the number one suspect in the assassination of the President . . . here he is . . . he is . . .' The voice describes the scene which is suddenly terminated in the violent gunshot from Ruby's pistol above the noise and press of the crowd in the basement.

MARGUERITE *springs round. She doesn't quite stand up. She looks desperate, as if light has hit her in between the eyes. The sound of the TV set whirs in the background.* MARGUERITE *is in pain. She is full of indignation and confusion. As she understands it some terrible hoax has been performed.*

Behind her on the TV set we can hear the name Jack Ruby being called out frequently. The Commentator pans desperately with his camera to get a shot of Ruby.

MARGUERITE *rears round, as if she is addressing the crowded room she is in, in the Six Flags Motel TV room.]*

MARGUERITE: ... That's him! ... That is the man! Do you hear me? I'm saying – he was the man in that photograph – ask Marina – ask her in Russian – she was there – I was told I was shown that man's face yesterday – last night – and I understand now – too clearly – you'd have to kill me too – I want to make a statement I want to make a statement! I'm Marguerite Oswald – I'm Lee Harvey's mother – I must be heard! The boy is a hero – not a murderer! [*She rises to her feet. She is alone on the stage. She looks so awfully alone and tired, and beaten down with her own imaginings real or unreal. Her heavy little body sweats. She shakes. She wants to cry. She wants to show. She must have her say. All those around her seem so alien. All they want to do is protect little* MARINA. *Only she speaks alone. A pause. After the silence, the darkness descends again.* MARGUERITE *like a heifer in pain somewhere reels in the blackness.]*

[*Out from the dark steps* MARINA. *This time she wears a simple neat cotton dress. She looks a little worried.*]

COMMISSION: Now Mrs Oswald it has been necessary to ask you back to Washington on account of the recent news story which I believe the *Houston Post* ran claiming your husband also tried to shoot Mr Richard Nixon. On the final day of your testimony, we asked you – do you remember any information or documents under your control or in your possession which would relate to or shed any light on the matters we have been examining which you have not presented here? And you replied 'I have nothing else. Everything has been taken from me'. Now Mrs Oswald it has been made necessary to recall you in the light of the new evidence.

MARINA: There were an awful lot of questions at that time, and I was very tired, and felt that I had told everything and I don't remember, I can't understand why I didn't mention this. It would have been better for me to mention it the first time than to make you all do more work on it. [*She steps back on the stage.*]

[*The lights come up. There is a bed.* LEE *is swiftly putting on a suit. Beside the bed is a bathroom door.*]

MARINA: . . . That's your suit Lee.

LEE: Yearh . . . sure it is.

MARINA: Is there a wedding?

LEE: There might be a funeral. [*He picks up his pistol from the bed. He carefully places it in his waistbelt.*]

MARINA: I don't understand you –

LEE: Nixon's coming into town this morning –

MARINA: Oh. So what?

LEE: So I'm going to see –

MARINA: Not with that gun –

LEE: I'm going to see Nixon – and will you leave me alone.

MARINA: Why the gun?

LEE: He's a bad man. That's why. [*He goes into the bathroom. He shuts the door. There is the sound of tap water running.*]

MARINA [*shouts*]: Lee you're not going – not like that – remember what I said after General Walker was shot at –

LEE [*off*]: No.

MARINA: I said I'd go right on down to the police and inform them of you. I can't live with you like this –

[*As* LEE *opens the door to come out,* MARINA *grabs at the handle. She pushes the door inwards.* LEE *tries to push the door outwards in its correct direction. They struggle.*]

LEE: Get away from that door –

MARINA: Not until you say you won't kill!

LEE: Marina – I'm warning you now! [*He manages to push the door out onto the stage.* MARINA *has to back away. As he comes out she lunges for the gun in his waistband. He fights with her.*]

MARINA: Lee ... don't ...

LEE: I want to be left! I ... [*He suddenly sags. He relaxes.* MARINA *takes the pistol. She looks at him.*] I won't fight with you –

MARINA: No. I'm a woman.

LEE: Give me my gun back.

[MARINA *throws it on the bed. He walks to it. She stands in front of him.*]

MARINA: You won't go out –

LEE: I won't go out – [*She lets him pick up the pistol.*]

MARINA: You'll stay home.

LEE: You are always getting in my way.

MARINA: You'll do what I ask.

LEE: I will not take the gun. But I am going out sometime – I'm going to go out and find if there is an appropriate opportunity and if there is I will use the pistol.

[*The stage darkens.* MARINA *comes back up front.*]

COMMISSION: Had it come to your attention Mrs Oswald that Mr Nixon was going to be in Dallas prior to that time?

MARINA: No, I did not.

COMMISSION: Had you seen anything in the newspapers or heard anything over the radio or television?

MARINA: No we didn't have TV I didn't see that in the newspaper. I did not think up this incident with Nixon myself.

COMMISSION: What do you mean by that Mrs Oswald?

MARINA: It might have been that he was just trying to test me. He was the kind of person who could try and wound somebody in that way. Possibly he didn't want to go out at all, but was just doing this all as a sort of joke, not really as a joke, but rather to simply wound me to make me feel bad.

COMMISSION: Do you recall the bathroom, how the door closes? Does it close into the bathroom on Neely Street or from the outside in?

MARINA: I don't remember now, I don't remember. I only remember that it was something to do with the bathroom.

COMMISSION: Did you lock him into the bathroom?

MARINA: I can't remember precisely.

COMMISSION: Do you recall how the locks were on the bathroom door there?

MARINA: I can't recall. We had several apartments and I might be confusing one apartment with the other.

COMMISSION: Is it your testimony that you made it impossible for him to get out if he wanted to?

MARINA: I don't remember.

COMMISSION: Did he try to get out of the bathroom?

MARINA: I remember that I held him.

COMMISSION: He is quite a big man and you are a small woman?

MARINA: He is not a big man, he is not strong.

COMMISSION: Did you have some fear that he would use the weapons against someone else?

MARINA: Of course, I was afraid.

COMMISSION: You thought that he might use his weapons against someone?

MARINA: After the incident with Nixon I stopped believing him.

COMMISSION: You what?

MARINA: I stopped believing him.

COMMISSION: Why?

MARINA: Because he wasn't obeying me any longer, because he promised and then he broke his promise.

All through this particular piece of recall evidence MARINA *seems ill at ease. It is obvious she doesn't know now in her own mind whether she invented this story or whether her mind at the earlier session with the Commission just couldn't focus on this Nixon episode.*

MARINA *stays where she is. The stage is now very bare. The lights come up. There stands* MARINA *on one side, on the other side stands* MARGUERITE. *They both stare out at the audience.* MARGUERITE *as of ever blurts out her own statement. She just stands there and says it as if she is waving a flag.*]

MARGUERITE: ... You see we have two sides here. It is a very serious charge, because no one saw him shoot at the President. And the Commission has come to the conclusion that Lee Harvey Oswald has shot President Kennedy, and he alone. Lee Harvey Oswald or Mr J.

Lee Rankin, or anyone in this room, could not have been in that many places in twenty-nine minutes time. It is utterly impossible. I have 1,500 letters sir – not just letters of sympathy, people that are investigating this. But he step by step has been taken, from what the reports said – that he was on the sixth floor, and then they saw him in the cafeteria drinking a Coca-Cola, and the President came. Then he had to leave the building. He had so many blocks to walk before he caught a bus. He had to board the bus, he had to pay his fare, he had to get out of the bus, then he walked a few blocks, then he caught a taxi-cab, then he paid the taxi man, then he walked a few blocks went to his home and got a coat. Then he walked a few more blocks and shot the policeman. Then he walked a few more blocks and he was in the theatre. In twenty-nine minutes time it cannot be done. [*She just stands there and says it. She is near calm. Not wholly so.*]

[MARINA *is very calm, cool and at ease. She doesn't seem very troubled by the breadth of the questions. Behind them both the stage is quite empty. Any small pieces of set have gone away. It is bleak and very very empty. Just the two women standing there.*]

COMMISSION: Mrs Oswald this question has already been asked you but I would like to ask it again. I gather that you have reached the conclusion in your own mind that your husband killed President Kennedy.

MARINA: Regretfully yes.

COMMISSION: During the weeks and months prior to the assassination – and I think this question has also been asked – did you ever at any time hear your late husband express any hostility toward President Kennedy?

MARINA: No.

COMMISSION: What motive would you ascribe to your husband in killing President Kennedy?

MARINA: As I saw the documents that were being read to me – I came to the conclusion that he wanted in any – by any means, good or bad, to get into history. But now that I have heard a part of the translation of some of the documents, I think that there was some political foundation to it, a foundation of which I am not aware.

COMMISSION: By that, do you mean that your husband acted in concert with someone else?

MARINA: No, only alone.

COMMISSION: You are convinced that his action alone, that he was influenced by no one else?

MARINA: Yes I am convinced.[1]

COMMISSION: Do you consider your husband a communist?

MARINA: He told me when we were in New Orleans that he was a communist, but I didn't believe him, because I said, 'what kind of a communist are you if you don't like the communists in Russia?'

COMMISSION: Did he like the communists in the United States?

MARINA: He considered them to be on a higher level and more conscious than the communists in Russia.

COMMISSION: Did you consider your husband a normal man in the usual sense of the word?

MARINA: He was always a normal man, but where it concerned his ideas, and he did not introduce me to his ideas, I did not consider him normal.

COMMISSION: Maybe I used the wrong terminology. Did you consider him mentally sound?

MARINA: Yes he was smart and capable. Only he did

1. The interchangeable sequence, pp, 18-20, can be placed here.

103

not use his capabilities in the proper direction – he was not deprived of reason – he was not a man deprived of reason.

[MARGUERITE *from the far side simply talks at the audience. She doesn't hear* MARINA. *She hears no one. Her words are very emotional. She finds meanings in almost the most trivial phrase.*]

MARGUERITE: ... So I am convinced my son, and my son alone, if he is involved, I am a human being, and I say my son could have shot the President, and he could have been involved. I am not the type mother to think that he is perfect and he could not do it. But I say he did not do it alone – if he did it. Because it is utterly impossible. And I do not believe my son did it. I think my son was framed because, gentlemen, – would his rifle be in the sixth floor window of the depository – unless you want to say my son was completely out of his mind. And yet there has been no statement to that effect. Wade has publicly said on television when it happened that he is sane, he is well reasoned, he knows what he did. And Lee never did break, with his black eyes. He kept saying that he was innocent. And yet in twelve hours time he was proven guilty. . . . That doesn't make sense to me an ordinary layman. So I have to consider who is involved. Now I am telling you that this girl was not happy with her situation. She had turned against me twice. . . . You, yourself, yesterday said that she testified that I told her to tear up the picture of Lee with those guns. God give me the Grace – I did no such thing. My testimony is true. So now she has lied there, I have found out. . . . And every evidence of any importance has come from this house. I have to face that. [*She is still now. She has finished. The mother stands rather limply. There are tears there. The voice is smashed and tired. The mother holds her face in her hands dramatically. Perhaps she means it to seem like that. She covers her eyes. She is empty and exhausted and bone still. That is all she can say.*]

[MARINA *waits for the question again. She is calm and tired. Her clothes are tidy and pretty. Her face is very American now. The makeup and the hairstyle.*]

COMMISSION: Now let me ask you one other question; assuming that this is correct, would you feel that there would be any less guilt in killing Governor Connally than in killing the President?

MARINA: I am not trying to vindicate or justify or excuse Lee as my husband. Even if he killed one of his neighbours, still it wouldn't make much difference – it wouldn't make any difference – a killing is a killing. I am sorry ...

APPENDIX

The Riddle of Oswald

The riddle of Oswald is a continuum. Little is definitive about this play. I have presented as well as I can all the facts which are known to this date. Since Kennedy's assassination time has both uncovered and destroyed many things. A number of important witnesses have died. At least two authors have written devastating analyses of the Warren Commission findings. There is a public outcry for an objective investigation of the Commission's Enquiry. The vital X-rays and photographs of Kennedy's body have yet to be seen by anyone outside the F.B.I. and members of the Kennedy family. I know too, by the time this play is published, Professor Richard Popkin will have made public a copy of the first F.B.I. report on the autopsy.[1] Above all, I am aware there is no final picture of the events to show. Once you have ploughed through everything, all the volumes of the Report, the articles, films and records, you are certainly left with doubt. This doubt is grit in the mind which will keep people for ever searching for the truth of the matter. For the most reasoned facts of the case one must go to Edward Jay Epstein and to Mark Lane for their intricate dismembering of the Warren Commission Report.

There is a great mystery here. If there is more than one assassin there is a conspiracy. After that, there is silence, there is a large blank wall against which Messrs Epstein, Lane, Popkin and Salandria untiringly beat with their questions. The ghost of Oswald, the sadness of the man, his loneliness, the bitter frustrated rancour in his heart kept me moving away

1. The report, now in the U.S. National Archives and hitherto unpublished, by F.B.I. agents Francis X. Oneill and James W. Sibert, who were present at the post-mortem, makes nonsense of the Commission's 'one bullet theory'.

from all the data, the endless escalation of doubt. In the beginning I thought it churlish of me to think about Oswald. We had lost Kennedy not Oswald, Oswald was not the hit of the century, President Kennedy was. ... After some months, I realized I couldn't accept the fact that Oswald was the lone assassin, but at the same time all the violent psychopathic seeds in a man which make for an assassin appeared to be there in Lee Oswald. Still I feel this, and the play is an attempt to grasp this problem – there is a missing fragment of authenticity about Oswald as an isolated man with a single purpose. Now I feel sure of one thing, and I hope the play brings this across – Oswald was a loner, he kept his reading and his studies to himself but never once, not once in his life, did he make a move on his own, by his own silent single choosing; always his actions were made not from aloneness, but out of reaction.

By reaction I mean rebound, to produce the reciprocal effect. It was reaction which made him join the Marines, it was reaction which sent him to Russia; there he asked one girl to marry him, he was refused, and he rebounded toward another, Marina, and was accepted. If he was not the single assassin, that day in Dallas, I feel he was motivated to join a conspiracy out of rebound against somebody. I believe it was in his makeup to respond to some stimulus, from someone, to actuate himself. I agree this can sound like wild surmise, as if I am falling into the same trap of speculators – the oil tycoon theory, the myth of the two Oswalds, or the insidious suggestion that Lyndon Baines Johnson was implicated. Any thought like this is glib speculation. It is as a playwright, not as a psycho-analyst, which I cannot pretend to be, nor as a riddle-solving student of data which is best left to the lawyers, that I am responding to this image of Oswald.

Edward Jay Epstein's book *Inquest* and Mark Lane's thorough investigation *Rush to Judgement* make very little effort to understand Oswald the man; their concern is to peel away the gauze curtains which surround the true facts. The Warren Commission has tried to compile a cold list of the man's life with dates and figures.[1] Occasionally people dismiss Oswald as an illiterate – his spelling, for instance – and in Gerald R. Ford's book *Portrait of the Assassin*, Ford sneers at the depth of Oswald's feelings when Oswald tried to commit suicide in Moscow. Ford quotes from Oswald's diary –

7.00 pm. I decide to end it. Soak wrist in cold water to numb pain. Then slash my left wrist. Then plunge wrist into bathtub of hot water. I think, 'when Rimma comes at eight to find me dead, it will be a great shock'. Somewhere a violin plays as I watch my life whirl away. I think to myself 'how easy to die' and 'a sweet death' (to violins). . . .

To Ford, a member of the Warren Commission, Oswald's attempt to kill himself was too 'complete with overtones of a Grade B movie with violins playing in the background' to take very seriously.

But this account of a suicide bid appears more genuine when you look at it closer. It is an image of a man observing himself as if he were himself. It is objective, theatrical and very, very cold. The hero of Norman Mailer's novel *An American Dream* hears the same light music as he considers self-destruction –

. . . but there is little that is sexual about suicide. It is a lonely landscape with the pale light of a dream and something is calling to you, a voice on the wind. Certain nights I would go leaden with dread because I could hear the chamber music tuning up, and near to pitch. (Yes, murder sounds like a symphony in your head, and suicide is a pure quartet.) . . .

At eighteen Oswald was in the Marines, he learnt Russian; at twenty he was in Minsk, in Russia; at twenty-one he had almost renounced both Russia and his own country, he had become a father, he read everything he could get his hands on from Norman Vincent Peale to Marx, and at twenty-two he was shuffling mysteriously from New Orleans to Mexico City, keeping box-number postal addresses and losing a job almost every six weeks. All right, he couldn't spell (but neither, for that matter, can a great number of distinguished writers!), the

1. Written by lawyers Wesley Liebeler and Alfred Goldberg.

photographs of his thin balding head make him look prematurely old, but Oswald isn't the stubbed out fag-end of a failure the American people at large want him to be.

Who is Lee Harvey Oswald? John Clellon Holmes, an American, began a remarkable article on Oswald with the words – 'Certainly I cannot have been alone in plodding through the entire Report for the sole purpose of understanding Oswald, and thus ridding myself of what threatened to become a plaguing obsession'. I gather Mr Holmes only tried the 800-page Report. I assure him the same preoccupation grows stronger after a haul through the entire twenty-six volumes, plus the Report, of the Warren Commission's testimonies and data. Holmes starts from the belief that Oswald was a psychopath, that he did the killing and did it alone, and Holmes asks – 'what was the specific need in this peculiar man that demanded this particular action?'

Rather like the gratuitous murder in Camus's *The Stranger*, Holmes anoints Oswald with a 'meaningless violence' and an existential 'gesture back at the reality he feels has excluded him'. Holmes asks us to look at a picture of an alienated, bleak individual as loveless and thwarted as any described in a Dostoyevsky novel. Now this picture does hold some credence, when you think of Oswald in the same light as that other young Texas Marine, who climbed up a tower with a small arsenal of weapons, and calmly sat down and killed fourteen people – fourteen little black unknowable shapes on the ground far below him. Like the unnamed hero of Barbusse's *L'Enfer*, Oswald is an anonymous man outside of society, sharply separated from the contact of the world's touch, with no identity – and in one single act he kicks back at the living world. The one violent act supplies him with space and distance and perspective – he now has an identity. Suddenly we are slap-bang in the middle of alienation – Reich, Van Gogh and Nijinsky; and President Kennedy is forgotten, and we have a convenient intellectual exegesis – those original doubts about the death of a President are assuaged again.

In the light of new evidence, Oswald, if he was up there

firing, was not alone. *The alienated man does not take a partner in a crime like this*. This is the difference, and it is very important, because nowhere is there anything but vague testimonial (*Hearings*, VII, pp. 410–18): Oswald had strange friends and political allies; yet if there were partners in the assassination, no matter how carefully they have been covered up, or had their tracks rubbed away, the 'strange friends and political allies' must indeed exist somewhere. I want to quote how Holmes sees Oswald: Holmes makes a humane portrait of the man before he canalizes Oswald into philosophic jargon –

... Rootless, traditionless, fatherless, unloved by his self-involved Mother, emotionally displaced by their peripatetic life together, moving restlessly from flat to flat, city to city, always crushingly alone, his hours occupied by TV and chance books, friendless and rejected ... the anonymous urban mass man, who almost always has the same blank, half scornful, sullen expression on his face ... cautious, irritable, hungry, masked ... happy nowhere ... psychic heat demanding ceaseless changes of mind ... hundreds of dreary 'official' letters to the Soviet authorities, the State department, the Navy department, the F.B.I. and almost everyone else, the sole reason for which was to define and get on the record his chameleon-like changes of status. Like many of us in this bureaucratized world, he searched for himself in his dossier.

One is made to concur with this; it seems accurate. Holmes has his finger on Oswald's pulse. Then he quotes Genet – 'I reject the world that has rejected me', and Holmes has gone off the track again; because such a lonely man who strikes back out of his wound to affirm his humanity does not conspire with others.

At root the 'a far mean streak' may be much more conspiratorial and mysterious than all his displaced feelings 'of indepence', or Oswald's hunger 'brought on by negleck'.

In this play LEE HARVEY OSWALD: A FAR MEAN STREAK OF INDEPENCE BROUGHT ON BY NEGLECK I have made a sparse documentation with film to make the facts clear and simple. I have taken slabs of question and answer verbatim from the volumes of the Commission Report – the testimonies from the mother and the wife – and I have dramatized episodes which both women describe. I have not besmirched or played around with the stories Marina and Marguerite have told. In writing the dialogue I have tried to be faithful to the words of the women in their testimonies. So doing – with Oswald centred between his wife and his mother – I have tried to reproduce, without any bias against character or credibility, the man Lee Harvey Oswald. It is the silence of the man which compels me to do this.

1 October 1966   MICHAEL HASTINGS